I0866633

TRIUMPH BOOKS

LEGENDARY

LEGENDARY

The 2008 Pittsburgh Steelers Defense, the Zone Blitz, and My Six Decades in the NFL

Dick LeBeau
with Scott Brown
and George Von Benko

TRIUMPH
BOOKS

First Triumph Books paperback edition 2025

Library of Congress Cataloging-in-Publication Data

Names: LeBeau, Dick, author. | Brown, Scott. | Von Benko, George, author.
Title: Legendary: the 2008 Pittsburgh Steelers defense, the zone blitz, and my six decades in the NFL / Dick LeBeau, with Scott Brown and George Von Benko.
Other titles: 2008 Pittsburgh Steelers defense, the zone blitz, and my 6 decades in the National Football League
Description: Chicago, Illinois: Triumph Books, [2024]
Identifiers: LCCN 2023049452 | ISBN 9781637273968 (cloth)
Subjects: LCSH: LeBeau, Dick. | Football coaches—Pennsylvania—Pittsburgh—Anecdotes. | Pittsburgh Steelers (Football team)—History—20th century. | Football—Defense. | Super Bowl (43rd: 2009: Tampa, Florida.) | Pro Football Hall of Fame (U.S.) |
National Football League. | BISAC: SPORTS & RECREATION / Coaching / Football | TRAVEL / United States / Northeast / Middle Atlantic (NJ, NY, PA)
Classification: LCC GV939.L375 A3 2024 | DDC 796.332/640974886—dc23/eng/20240212
LC record available at https://lccn.loc.gov/2023049452

This book is available in quantity at special discounts for your group or organization. For further information, contact:

Triumph Books LLC
814 North Franklin Street
Chicago, Illinois 60610
(312) 337-0747
www.triumphbooks.com

Printed in U.S.A.
ISBN: 978-1-63727-944-1

Design by Patricia Frey

To, my mother, Beulah, who became an angel for the second time in 2009 when she passed away at the age of 96. Her love shaped me in every way possible.

To every player I ever coached, you truly made it a great day to be alive. I thank all of you.

To Kevin Colbert, who assembled the 2008 team that is so near and dear to me. Kevin was a terrific general manager and is an even better person.

With 35 seconds left in Super Bowl XLIII, Pittsburgh Steelers head coach Mike Tomlin gathered all of the defensive players around him as we prepared to kick off. He looked each player in the face as he spoke. "I have seen some great defenses in this league, Super Bowl-champion defenses. You guys have had a terrific season. You have played great defense all year. If you make this one last stop right now, you will become a legendary *defense."*

Contents

Forewords *by James Harrison and Troy Polamalu* **17**

Introduction *by Scott Brown* **21**

1. Houston Has a Problem **31**
2. Dynamic Duo **43**
3. Not-So Brotherly Love in Philly **53**
4. Blitzing Baltimore **65**
5. Ben Comes Up Big **75**
6. Coaching for and against the Bengals **83**
7. Big Blue Battle **95**
8. Election Day in D.C. **105**
9. Peyton's Place **119**
10. Super Bowl Dress Rehearsal **129**
11. Hello Again, Cincinnati **139**
12. Redemption in New England **151**
13. Townsend Steps Up against Lone-Star Rival **161**
14. Another Steelers–Ravens Classic **173**
15. Singing the Holiday Blues **183**
16. Hollywood (Regular-Season) Ending **193**
17. Charging Forward **201**
18. The Legend of Troy **211**
19. Guardian Angels and a Super Finish **221**

Afterword *by Scott Brown* **233**

Appendix I: Author Tributes **237**

Appendix II: The 2008 Pittsburgh Steelers Defense **243**

About the Authors **249**

Foreword

Every coach is different and coaches in different ways. You may be willing to do some of the same things for them that you would do for other coaches. The big difference with Dick LeBeau is guys loved him, and he coached with love. Everything that he did was essentially in the approach that you would have toward your son if you were trying to coach him in a loving manner. That was one of the big things about Coach that a lot of people don't know or understand unless you were coached by him.

I tell people all the time if it wasn't for Dick LeBeau and Keith Butler, there would be no James Harrison. I had been cut by the Steelers three times before re-signing with them right before 2004 training camp. When I went in that year, I was down to my last NFL chance. At least, that is the way I looked at it. I decided to take the time to be a true professional and actually learn the defense. The hardest thing for me when I first got there in 2002 as an undrafted free agent was trying to master the playbook. The linebacker coach I had wasn't that great to me, to be 100 percent honest. That's why I am so grateful to Dick and Keith. They were exactly what I needed at that time.

Keith could teach you that position inside out, left to right, up and down, and Dick LeBeau didn't cuss you out and make you feel terrible if you made a mistake. Instead, you felt terrible because you made a mistake and you let his defense down. His approach was, "That last play, let it go. Let's get the next one." He instilled so much confidence in his players.

The biggest thing was respect. Coach LeBeau, as far as how he talked to you and the mannerisms that he used, treated an All-Pro and a nobody with the same respect. That clicked with a lot of guys. You have a lot of coaches who talk differently to younger guys than they do their star players. Now I'm not saying he gave a rookie the same liberties he gave an All-Pro player. You were not going to get a pass when you walked into a meeting a minute late if you were a rookie. But even then he was not going to jump on a rookie's neck. He was going to talk to him afterward, pull him to the side, and be upfront with him.

I had the utmost trust in him as a coach for a simple reason: his defense worked. When you played that defense exactly how it was supposed to be played, nothing could go wrong. It was a very complex defense, believe me. If one person did something wrong, you could strike up the band. But when you had all 11 guys on the same page, it was a hard defense to beat.

—***James Harrison*** *made the Steelers as an undrafted free agent and became one of the most unlikely success stories in NFL history. A five-time Pro Bowl selection, Harrison won two Super Bowls with the Steelers, and his 100-yard interception return in Super Bowl XLIII is still the longest in the game's illustrious history. The outside linebacker won the NFL Defensive Player of the Year award in 2008 and remains the only undrafted free agent to ever win it. The Steelers inducted him into their Hall of Honor in October 2023.*

Foreword

It's funny how folks describe my career as the first year being very challenging and then changing from then on, which kind of coincided with Coach LeBeau's first year back with the Steelers in 2004. Obviously, the addition of him in my life at that time was very significant. He gave me a lot of leeway. What is not talked about as much is his giving me a lot of responsibility as well, and with that responsibility comes a lot of accountability. He absolutely had so much trust in me, but he had the trust in me learning a lot of different positions, me being able to move around, and me being used as that chess piece. That's a really wonderful combination. You see a lot of these connections that coaches really have with athletes—whether it's in basketball, baseball, or whatever sport.

Coach LeBeau is that person to me and not only to me, but also, to be perfectly frank, to every single player that he's ever coached. Everything came together in 2008, when he had an all-time great defense. James Harrison won NFL Defensive Player of the Year, and I don't think I've ever seen an outside linebacker do the things that he did that year. We just had so much talent across the board, and it was not magazine-cover talent. It was Pittsburgh-style talent that went about its business and didn't really care about the spotlight and really took on the personality of Coach LeBeau.

He epitomizes everything as a man that I wanted to be. Among many amazing father figures in my life, he's a great father figure to me. For the period in my life that I was going through—the transition from college to the NFL and to adulthood and marriage—Coach LeBeau was definitely a huge foundation for me. Aside from that, he represents the whole defense and the team from that era, too.

What I've always said to people is I don't think anybody, who wasn't an owner of a team, has been a part of NFL football longer than he was. He played with legends. He played against legends. The same with coaching. He just has a profound perspective on the game. The Lombardi Trophy should be named after him. I truly mean that because nobody has had the experience that he's had, nobody has had that length of commitment, and those who know him often love him more than their own families. I can't imagine anybody like him ever. It's a blessing that I'm a part of his life, and he's a part of my life.

*—**Troy Polamalu** spent his entire 12-year career as a strong safety for the Pittsburgh Steelers. He was the point of the spear for the Steelers' great 2008 defense. An eight-time Pro Bowl and six-time All-Pro selection, he was inducted into the Pro Football Hall of Fame in 2020, his first year of eligibility, and introduced by LeBeau, who is also in the Pro Football Hall of Fame.*

Introduction

Dick LeBeau had spent almost 50 years in the NFL by 2008. He had seen everything during a playing career that led him to the Pro Football Hall of Fame followed by an equally decorated coaching career.

Or had he?

As the Pittsburgh Steelers were preparing for Super Bowl XLIII—and still in Pittsburgh since there were two weeks before the big game—LeBeau took a closer look at the numbers. LeBeau set statistical goals for his defenses to reach every game. He gave those benchmarks to his players before a game and reviewed how many of those they had hit after a game. Given how often the Steelers exceeded those benchmarks in 2008, it hardly surprised LeBeau that they also set the NFL standard in so many statistical categories.

Indeed, prior to the season, LeBeau had outlined his goal in 11 categories that he dubbed "critical areas." They were the average in each category of the top 10 defenses from the previous season.

The Steelers finished first in the NFL in nine of the 11 statistical categories. They exceeded LeBeau's goal in all 11 of them. "It's overwhelming," LeBeau said. "When you put those numbers like they put up and where they finished in terms of every other defense in the league, I had never seen anything like it and I had kept the stats for 25, 30 years."

Category	Average	NFL Rank	LeBeau's Statistical Goal
Points	13.9	1	17
Total Yards	237.2	1	300
Yards Per Play	3.9	1	4.7
Passing Yards	156.9	1	200
Passing Yards Per Attempt	4.3	1	5.7
Rushing Yards	80.3	2	100
Yards Per Carry	3.5	1	3.7
Sacks	51 total	2	48 total
Yards Per Catch	9.4	1	10
Third-Down Defense	31.4 percent	1	37.5 percent
Red Zone Defense	33.3 percent	1	47 percent

To see how that defense stacked up historically, LeBeau crunched numbers from some of the great Detroit Lions defenses he played on in the 1960s. "I looked at how many points we gave up and how many yards we gave up. I said, 'Hell, these guys played like we did in 1963,' which was a totally different style of play," LeBeau said. "Vince Lombardi ran the ball 65 percent of the time and threw it 35 percent of the time. They were the standard for the NFL, and everyone was copying what they did. Now teams throw it 65 to 70 percent of the time. That is when it hit me how special this group was. I don't know if anyone's going to come close to these numbers again."

Numbers only tell part of the story of the Steelers' 2008 defense with the journey making the group as unique as the destination. That unit came together for so many reasons. There were the Thursday night get-togethers hosted by defensive captain James Farrior. The mornings of LeBeau greeting them with his signature, "It's a great day to be alive!" no matter how brilliant or how sub-standard they were the day before. The total buy-in of players—all from different backgrounds.

The result was a symphony on grass, 11 parts moving together, players routinely showing that—as great as they were separately—they were even better as one. If the transcendence of that unit had to be distilled to one play, well, that's an easy one. It happened during the Super Bowl—and is the greatest play that LeBeau has ever seen.

There is a truism among sportswriters that when the material is so good: just get out of the way. That certainly applies to James Harrison's 100-yard interception for a touchdown in Super Bowl XLIII against the Arizona Cardinals. Starting with the week of practices, here is the play as recalled by Harrison himself and his teammates.

* * *

James Harrison: "At the beginning of one of the [Super Bowl] practices in Florida, Coach LeBeau gave us the percentages of a team winning if they scored a defensive touchdown in the Super Bowl. It was something close to 90 percent. That week every time we practiced—seven on seven, nine on seven, even one-on-one—if a dude got a pick, everybody ran back and made like they were throwing a block or threw a block and we would go the whole length of the field. Even if we were doing red zone and got an interception, we would run the whole length of the field."

Bryant McFadden: "We were catching interceptions in practice in Tampa, getting ready for the Super Bowl, but we weren't returning them. I would catch the football and just stop and get ready for the next practice rep. They were like, 'Stop this. When you catch the ball, act like you're in a live game. Score and find someone to block.' It didn't matter where we were on the field. We were trying to score and we were looking for someone to block."

Ryan Clark: "The only time Coach LeBeau ever got mad at us that year was at practice for the Super Bowl on Wednesday. We were getting interceptions and turnovers, but we weren't returning them. Thursday he comes in and shows every turnover from practice and he's yelling at us about transitioning and becoming offense on interceptions and turnovers. The rest of the week [when] somebody got an interception, we jumped into it and started blocking, and that guy scored."

Ben Roethlisberger: "I do remember one of the practices leading up to the Super Bowl, a turnover happened, and a few guys blocked—but not everybody—and I remember LeBeau and then Tomlin jumped on the bandwagon. They made those guys either start over or do the drill over and they got on them for not doing it. After that every time the ball was turned over every player, even guys on the sideline, were running after the ball. It was unbelievable."

The Arizona Cardinals trailed 10–7 in the second quarter but looked poised to take the lead—and momentum—into halftime. After a Pittsburgh Steelers turnover, quarterback Kurt Warner drove the Cardinals to the 1-yard line. Arizona took its final timeout with 18 seconds left. Figuring the Cardinals would not risk getting stopped on a running play, LeBeau called a max blitz.

LaMarr Woodley: "The play was called 'Dog Rush One' with James and me both rushing. I did what I was supposed to do, and James, like a veteran, did what he had seen [and dropped into coverage]. Overall, it was smart because if I was on that side, hell, I would have rushed. It was my second year in the league, and I didn't have the pull to be overriding Dick LeBeau. I put a little pressure on Kurt Warner, and he threw the ball. I heard the crowd roar and I turned around and looked. I see James Harrison with the ball running."

Troy Polamalu: "We had seen this play so many times, and to be honest, Hines Ward had scored on this play so many times throughout his career. It was really kind of a hot check when you were in Cover Zero. I remember being man to man on the tight end and I saw the receiver stacked on the other side of the formation. The funny thing is I remember thinking to myself, *I wonder if I could just go all the way over there and try to sit on this route.* But my first thought after that was: *if I don't make that play, Coach LeBeau is going to be really pissed at me.* I didn't run over there and kind of hovered over my guy, knowing the play is going to be on the other side, and obviously Harrison made that play."

Harrison: "That's one of the things that Coach gave us liberty to do. He said, 'I'm not out there with you. I don't see what you see. I've got a different view.' Well, I see that we're getting to Kurt Warner a step too late. We get there, and he's throwing the ball as we hit him. I'm like, 'Shit, we're calling a max blitz. Somebody's going to be free. I can affect one pass. They can't take a chance to run.' I dropped to cover the flat end because that was the closest thing to me, the only thing I could affect. I knew I needed to step at the tackle to get him to step toward me like he was going to block me. That way [Lawrence] Timmons would be able to get through free. If Timmons is getting through free, Kurt can't hold the ball, and then me dropping is not a big deal. I dropped, and Kurt couldn't see me and he threw the ball to me."

Farrior: "I'm dropping back and I'm in the end zone a little bit. I saw James rush, but I didn't see him back out. I saw him catch the ball, and he was in front of me. [Cardinals wide receiver Anquan] Boldin was behind me. He started running. So, I was trying to shield Boldin off, and Boldin ended up pulling me down by my neck brace. I was just watching the play after that."

As Harrison started running the other way, LeBeau yelled from the Steelers sidelines to get down. He did not want the Steelers to fumble the ball back to the Cardinals. Running right behind Harrison, cornerback Deshea Townsend tried to get the bigger player to hand him the ball.

Harrison: "It felt like I was fighting with him for like 15, 20 seconds. I'm like, 'Go block somebody.'"

Polamalu: "It was like an Ed Reed thing. If you're not going to score, then give the ball to somebody that could, and we didn't have confidence that Harrison could run from end zone to end zone and break that many tackles."

Ike Taylor: "I kept telling James to throw me the ball. Little did I know me running behind him asking him for the ball was one of the first blocks."

Woodley: "My first thought was: *Turn around and block somebody.* The first person I saw to block was Kurt Warner. I made a decision that I'm not blocking him because he's slow and he's not going to get to the play. I bumped him out of the way a little bit and ran on. The running back from the Cardinals was [Tim] Hightower. So I pushed him and then I looked back. James was still running."

As Harrison picked up blocks and steam, LeBeau started yelling, "Run, James. Run!"

Brett Keisel: "I remember saying, 'Let's go, Deebo!' I kept yelling it at him as we were running down the sidelines. It seemed like there was red everywhere, but anytime someone was about to get him, there was a Steeler there to block."

Farrior: "There's like three seconds left, and he's at the 50-yard line. I'm thinking he needs to get out of bounds so we can get a field goal. The clock runs out and I'm like, *Well, damn, he has to score now.* I'm watching thinking, *They're going to get him, they're going to get him.* I think Woodley was the person that made the last block before he tumbled into the end zone after [Larry] Fitzgerald jumped on his back. That was something else to just watch."

Woodley: "I only had a little gas left in the tank for maybe one more block. I turned on the little speed I had left and made the little final push. Luckily, James hurdled over my feet, and I didn't trip him, and he went on in for the touchdown. I laid on the ground and watched him because that was all I had."

Harrison completed one of the greatest and most improbable plays in Super Bowl history when he collapsed into the end zone with no time remaining in the second quarter. He stayed on the ground as the play was reviewed and then confirmed as a touchdown for the Steelers.

Farrior: "When he laid out on the field, I was like, *Ah, shoot, he may not even make it back out after halftime.* We had to give him oxygen. I don't think he said three words the whole halftime."

Harrison: "When I fell, the first thing to hit was my head. I went to lift my head to get up and go, and then it popped again. I was like, 'No, go get the trainer.' Plus, I couldn't breathe so there was no chance of me getting up. I jammed my neck, and it was misaligned. It took my chiropractor damn near 12, 18 months to get that mother to pop back out."

Polamalu: "The runback was incredible. It not only showed the tremendous amount of shape that everybody was in but the fortitude to be able to continue to push through that. The play was the culmination of a lot of instinctual things. It was the sixth sense for the coaches to really stress [blocking after an interception in practice]. It was the sixth sense for Harrison to fall into that zone. Had I followed my instinct, I would have ruined the play. I probably would have hit Harrison, and we both would have dropped the interception or something like that."

Aaron Smith: "From a team standpoint, it might be the greatest team football play in history. We never felt like we were down and out and going to give up. James makes a play, and most people think, *Oh, just get out of the half.* Everybody found someone to block and did it. It didn't matter who was scoring the touchdown. We didn't care who got the sacks. We didn't care who got the tackles. We didn't care who got the interceptions. We just wanted to win. That sums up our whole season as a defense right there."

* * *

The story behind that play *is* the story of the Steelers' 2008 defense. The roots—of both—are like those of a tree, spreading far and wide. This book ties everything together, chronicling a magical season through the eyes of the players and the coach who loved them like sons as they loved him like a father. *Legendary* is about personalities and posterity. It is about James Harrison's remarkable rise from obscurity, Troy Polamalu's rock-star appeal that fit his playing style but belied his humility, and James Farrior proving that Ben Roethlisberger was not the only great signal caller on the Steelers' roster. And that is just a short list.

Most of all it is about a coach and players willing to fight for each other. Harrison's 100-yard interception return is the best example of that but only one of many.

Three months earlier, the Steelers stopped the New York Giants from their 1-yard line when a touchdown looked like a *fait accompli.* The defense stuffed 260-pound running back Brandon Jacobs on three consecutive carries. Among those leading the charge was defensive end Aaron Smith.

Less than a week earlier, his young son had been diagnosed with leukemia. Smith rarely left Children's Hospital of Pittsburgh that week. He did not even know if he was going to play against the Giants until the morning of the game. Yet there he was, when he needed his brothers as much as they needed him, refusing to cede so much as an inch. That, as much as Harrison's interception return for a touchdown in the Super Bowl or one of Polamalu's how-did-he-do-that plays, shaped the legacy of the 2008 Steelers.

—*Scott Brown*

1

Houston Has a Problem

You can't talk about the linebackers on the 2008 Pittsburgh Steelers' defense without starting with the two Jameses: Farrior and Harrison.

Harrison has such a unique story, one that is always worth re-telling. His name came up less than a week before we were going to training camp in 2004. I had never heard of him. He had already been released three times by the Steelers, and even though I was the defensive coordinator, this was my first year back with the Steelers after coaching in Pittsburgh from 1992 to 1996.

We had set our training camp roster, but outside linebacker Clark Haggans broke a small bone in his hand while lifting weights during his last workout before reporting to St. Vincent College in Latrobe, Pennsylvania. That left us short a linebacker for training camp. We were in a staff meeting, and somebody said, "What about James Harrison?"

I said, "I don't know him. Ask the coaches who were here when James had time here." Keith Butler had coached him and spoke favorably of him and his football ability. I said, "We've got a coach here who says he's got upside."

We got into camp and every day we'd go over personnel. There's nothing else to do at training camp at night. One meeting I said, "Who's this 92?"

Butler said, "Well, that's James Harrison."

"Well, I've been watching him," I said. "I haven't seen anybody block him yet in any of the drills or any of the team activities. This guy has got an innate ability to get leverage and maintain it."

I coached all these guys as though they were not only going to make the team, but also become starters. I didn't care whether the guys were drafted, free agents, or just balancing out the roster. The league is full of guys who were drafted. It's also full of guys who really weren't highly regarded coming out of college. But they got into a camp, went to the right environment, and they produced. I never paid too much attention to where we got players when I was coaching. I just watched them practice and play and I made my decisions based on that. Harrison was an NFL player from the first two practices that I saw him. Nobody could block him, and he was strong, quick, and tough. Those are pretty good credentials for outside linebackers.

I kept singing his praises, and Harrison really started contributing on special teams, which is the best way an unheralded guy can make a team. If someone had asked on the first day of training camp, "Do you think Harrison will make it?" I don't think you would have found anybody who would have said yes because he had already been released so many times before.

I also think Harrison would say he had learned some things about fitting in with his teammates a little better. I think he learned that what he had been doing wasn't working, and he got a little smarter in terms of interacting with teammates and being more of a team guy and getting with the program a little bit more. That made it easier to argue for him. He made the team mostly because of what he did on special teams in the preseason.

In the middle of November, we played at Cleveland. The Browns had a real feisty, competitive running back by the name of William Green. He unwittingly played a major role in getting Harrison the only audition he needed to show he could be much more than a special teams player. During pregame warm-ups Green came into our stretching drill and started yapping at Joey Porter, who was competitive and didn't need too much instigation to retaliate. Porter got up and bumped him, and the two started throwing blows. We're not even out of stretching, and both players got thrown out of the game. That meant we were without our starting outside linebacker.

Butler had gone to the locker room before all of this. When I found him, I said, "Go get Harrison. Find out what he's comfortable with. He's starting this game, and I don't want to call anything the first couple of drives that he's not real secure with."

Butler laughed.

But I told him, "No, this is not a joke."

He said, "What happened?"

"They threw Joey out of the game. He's out, and Harrison's in."

Butler talked to Harrison and told me, "He said he's okay with any of the basic stuff. He's ready to go."

Harrison just played lights out that day, and we knew right then that we had us a real football player. I knew this kid was going to be a starting outside linebacker. Now did I know he was going to be the Most Valuable Player in the league? No. Did I know that he was going to make the most exciting defensive play that I've ever seen? I didn't know that either. It's a one-in-a-million story.

Of course, Harrison had to bide his time before becoming a full-time starter. Porter was an excellent player in front of him and one of the driving forces behind us winning Super Bowl XL. He left after the 2006 season, signing a big contract with the Miami Dolphins. As much as I hated seeing Porter go, I was very comfortable with Harrison starting. Yeah, he was green as grass, and I knew he had some work to do, but he obviously put that work in based on his first season as a starter. Harrison made the Pro Bowl and was voted by his teammates as the Steelers' 2007 MVP. He staged a heck of a national coming out party that season in early November. Harrison wrecked the Baltimore Ravens' offense in a *Monday Night Football* game with three-and-half sacks, three forced fumbles, a fumble recovery, and an interception in our 38–7 win at Heinz Field. He just continued to build on that and turned himself into a great player.

He was a great teammate, too. Once Harrison got comfortable with what he was doing, he ended up teaching the rookie outside linebackers a lot of stuff through the years because he understood the defense so well.

No one knew it better than Farrior, a captain and our defense's unquestioned leader. He was the hub of the wheel, and part of it was the position that he played. He was setting the defense and the voice that the defense heard. He never missed a doggone play. He was there every game, every snap. He has to be one of the best free-agent signings not just in Steelers but also in NFL history.

I worked him out at Virginia when he was coming out for the NFL draft in 1997 and I really liked him. After one running drill, I looked at my stopwatch and said, "I might have made a mistake." I started looking at the scouts around me, and they all had the same time. He was faster than hell and he's not small. He was a real tough and aggressive guy.

The New York Jets took him with the eighth overall pick in the draft that year, and I could not believe they let him leave after the 2001 season. All I knew is that when I returned to Pittsburgh in 2004, I was going to have a good inside linebacker. It did not take long for me to realize that he was going to be great. In 2004 Farrior had such a good season that he finished second for the NFL Defensive Player on the Year award. He made 95 tackles with four interceptions and three sacks and showed what a complete player he was in the middle of our defense.

He was very quiet actually, but when he spoke, everybody listened. He had the presence of a football player, and teams couldn't block him. They couldn't cut him off because he was deceptively fast, and he had great linemen in front of him who would hold their positions and give him room to roam.

If you looked at the tackle sheet, it almost always started with Farrior week in and week out. He was like Troy Polamalu on a lesser scale. He didn't make the interceptions and touchdowns like defensive backs did because of his position, but he was as instinctive as Polamalu in terms of where the ball was going. He just had the ability to decipher the flow and blocking pattern of the play almost instantly. He would get there before his intended blocker would and make the play. We had guys like that virtually at every position, and Farrior was our leader, our captain. He was the signal-caller and the only guy who spoke in the huddle.

I felt good about our defense going into 2008, especially after we made it through training camp and the preseason in good health. The guys were really dialed in because we felt we had some unfinished business. We had won the AFC North in Mike Tomlin's first season as head coach but lost in the playoffs to the Jacksonville Jaguars. They ran the ball on us in their 31–29 overtime win, and that did not sit well with anyone. Going into training camp, we talked about not finishing the year like we had the year before.

I liked how the players responded, but I still had reason to be a little anxious going into the season opener against the visiting Houston Texans. You never know what to expect in your opener. It's the first time that you've played the full 60 minutes. You don't really have any game film to study on the other team. You just have last year's and a little bit from their regular guys playing in preseason games, so there is that unknown.

Houston quarterback Matt Schaub was in his second year of running the Texans' offense after coming over in a trade with the Atlanta Falcons, and they were optimistic that he'd be ready to roll. The game plan was to blitz and attack them—even more than our already heavy blitz tendency. Schaub hadn't been running the offense that long, and the Texans were a team in transition, so we went after them.

As it turned out, we could not have scripted a better start to the season. We treated our fans to a 38–17 win at Heinz Field, and the game was not that close. Houston couldn't get going at all, and we completely controlled the game from the outset.

The Texans got the ball first and managed a couple of first downs. On fourth and 1 from our 48-yard line, Schaub tried to sneak for the first down. Our nose tackle Casey Hampton—immovable as he was unblockable in the middle of the defense—stopped him short of the sticks. From there it was all Steelers.

The offense went right down the field, and Willie Parker capped an eight-play drive with a seven-yard touchdown run. Houston had 15 total yards on its next two possessions, one of which ended in an interception for our first takeaway of the season. We scored touchdowns on our first three possessions to make it 21–0 before any late-arriving fans had gotten to their seats.

Parker was coming off a broken leg he suffered near the end of the 2007 season, and we were all kind of crossing our fingers a little bit. He was a great, explosive back and had been a big part of the 2005 team that won the Super Bowl. He ended up with 25 carries for 138 yards. It was very reassuring to all of us to see him flash that kind of form.

It was 21–3 at the half, and we scored twice in the third quarter to make it 35–3. Coach Tomlin took Ben Roethlisberger, our starting quarterback, out of the game early in the fourth quarter. That's the kind of game that it was, and those are rare in the NFL. The league just isn't put together that way with its emphasis on parity and how closely matched most teams are.

One adverse situation cropped up before the game had been put away. With seven minutes left in the second quarter, Houston sacked Roethlisberger, and Mario Williams picked up a fumble. A long return and a facemask penalty put the Texans on our 12-yard line. In sudden change situations like that, I always stressed that you have no control how you get on the field. You have to control how you come off the field. Make them kick field goals if they get a good break or make a big play. The players heard that in the first defensive meeting they attended every spring, and the 2008 group wasted little time turning those words into action.

Our line just engulfed the Texans, who ran three plays for minus-six yards. Talk about a response. Houston settled for a field goal to cut the lead to 21–3, and that was really Houston's last chance to be successful. The Texans finished the game with 234 total yards of offense, but most of those—and their two touchdowns—came after the game was completely out of reach. Schaub completed 25 of 33 passes, but we sacked him five times, including three by Harrison. The Texans were just three of 10 on third down, and, of course, our fourth-down stop early set the tone.

You can't draw any sweeping conclusions from a first game, especially one that was as lopsided as this. It did confirm how good I felt about our linebackers and not just the two Jameses. Larry Foote was the yin to Farrior's yang—as chatty as Farrior was quiet, but his stellar play alongside Farrior at inside linebacker spoke the loudest. He was an extremely intelligent, gifted athlete who had quickness and anticipation. By just knowing the formation tendencies, he would recognize how the play would initially unfold, often beat the blocking scheme, and get to where he had to. He was a very consistent and productive player.

He and Farrior were quick laterally and speedy with very in-close quickness. They could get to any hole at the line of scrimmage. What made them such a great tandem is that they were interchangeable because of their skillsets.

The Houston game also showed why we were so excited about a couple of second-year linebackers in Lawrence Timmons and LaMarr Woodley. They had been our first- and second-second draft picks in 2007, and I had really wanted each of them. Timmons was really athletic on the inside and gave us another starting caliber player at inside linebacker.

Woodley had been a defensive end at the University of Michigan. You could see he was going to be a really good pass rusher and strong against the run, but he had played in a 4-3 defense, and we were going to ask him to get off in space a little bit as an outside linebacker and get into pass coverage. I spent a lot of time evaluating him on that, but I watched his feet playing from a 4-3 with his pass rush, and he was such a coordinated athlete and a big man. I had experience taking 4-3 rush ends (if they weren't 6-foot-3 and 310 pounds or real thick guys) and then having a lot of success with them transferring over to a 3-4 outside linebacker.

Woodley was heavily muscled, but I watched enough tape on him that I thought his pass-rushing skills far outweighed anything that would be a liability from him in space. After we drafted him, I carefully watched to see what he did when he dropped into pass coverage. In our second preseason game in 2007 against the Green Bay Packers, Woodley ended up on a tight end who was running a stretch route. He ran stride for stride with the guy and, when the ball came, he reached up and had the athletic skills and hand-eye coordination to just knock the ball away like a defensive back would do. I turned to Butler on the sidelines and said, "Well, Coach, I think we've had all of our questions answered whether Woodley can play off the line of scrimmage enough to fit our situation." From that day on, I never worried about him being able to play outside linebacker in our defense.

Woodley, who moved into the starting lineup in 2008 after Haggans left in free agency, showed how complete of a linebacker he was in the win against the Texans. He intercepted Schaub to set up our second touchdown. He also recovered a fumble and had a sack. He was as much of a force as Harrison, and neither played the whole game.

I started to think that we could have another combination of outside pass rushers like Greg Lloyd and Kevin Greene and later Porter and Haggans. To me that was a pretty pleasant thought because in the 3-4 if you've got outside linebackers who can pass rush, you're probably going to have a pretty good defense. One thing about my philosophy was that I called defenses to put players in position to win their matchups. If you were blitzing and you got one on one, I expected you to win. One thing I knew after the first game of the season was that I would not have to worry about that with Harrison and Woodley.

Harrison's Last Chance

After signing with the team as a free agent in 2002, James Farrior was on the Pittsburgh Steelers, and his first year coincided with that of an undrafted free agent trying to make the team. His name was James Harrison, and he was…well…interesting. "He was a good player, but I thought he was crazy because of some of the stuff he would do," Farrior said. "One play in practice, he didn't really know what he was doing and he just stopped in the middle of the play and was like, 'I can't do this shit. Y'all get me out of here.' I was like, '*What the hell are you doing?* If you don't do anything else, just go full speed and hit something. They'll coach you up, but they want to see effort. They want to see you going full speed. They don't want to see you slowing down and not doing anything.'

"One of the scouts asked me, 'What's the deal with James Harrison? He seems kind of crazy. I don't know if he wants to make the team. Some of the stuff he's doing is going to get him cut.'"

And it did. Three times by the Steelers and once by the Baltimore Ravens. "He would be in weight room and telling people that this machine was his and that machine was his. "I was like, 'Dude, this guy's crazy,'" said Brett Keisel, who was drafted by the Steelers the same year they signed Harrison as an undrafted free agent. "James was honest. If he didn't understand something, he would say, 'I don't get that' or 'This doesn't make sense to me.'"

Harrison was down to his last chance—at least in his mind—when the Steelers re-signed him right before training camp in 2004 because of an injury starting outside linebacker Clark Haggans sustained while lifting weights. That coincided with Dick LeBeau's return for a second stint as the Steelers' defensive coordinator. Harrison took to his and second-year linebacker coach Keith Butler's coaching and made the 53-man roster. He never looked back, becoming one of the greatest success stories in NFL history relative to such humble beginnings.

Harrison had resolved to walk away from football if it didn't work out in Pittsburgh that year. "That would have meant that it wasn't meant for me because I had gone and gave it everything I had," he said. "I would have been working a regular job like everyone else. There's nothing wrong with that."

—S.B.

2

Dynamic Duo

I met a soft-spoken safety by the name of Troy Polamalu for the first time after returning to the Pittsburgh Steelers in 2004 for a second stint as defensive coordinator. I certainly knew of him. I had scouted him coming out of Southern Cal, and he was one in a million in terms of athleticism, stopping and starting, and those types of things.

The Steelers had traded up in the first round of the 2003 NFL Draft to take him, but he played primarily on special teams as a rookie and did not even start a game. He broke out in a big way in his second season, starting every game and making the first of many Pro Bowls. His emergence was a major reason why we went 15–1 and reached the 2004 AFC Championship Game. Polamalu has been generous—maybe too generous—when talking about the impact I had on his career. He had everything you needed to be a transcendent player.

He had unbelievable acceleration and had what I called applicable speed. He was plenty fast in just a straight 40-yard dash. But from play recognition to defensive application, he was as quick as anyone I ever saw and he weighed 220 pounds. So when he got there, he was carrying a sizable punch with him. You didn't need any expertise in football to see that this guy was a little bit different.

One thing that helped in our relationship: I was a defensive back myself, and my primary coaching experience had been coaching defensive backs. I spent a lifetime looking at what worked and what didn't work for me and for my teammates. By the time I got into coaching, I thought that I was pretty much ready to help any young man who wanted to improve himself football skill-wise.

I hadn't paid much attention to Polamalu's rookie season. I was an assistant head coach for the Buffalo Bills in 2003, and we did not play the Steelers that season. They had played him at a bunch of positions, and when I returned to Pittsburgh, we just narrowed it down a little bit for him. We wanted him to get comfortable with what he was doing and let him play. I knew some things to do and some things not to do. I just saw a couple of things that Polamalu wasn't doing. They were very minor, and once Polamalu took care of those, it seemed to just nudge him to another level. Man, he went crazy and he tore the league up.

As instinctive a player as Polamalu was, he also put in the work. A lot of his success came from film study. I would see Polamalu before the ball was snapped—when somebody would go in motion or adjust the formation—and he knew where the ball was going. He was on his way before they even snapped the damn thing. He was born to play football, no question about it.

I think Polamalu would be the first to say that Ryan Clark, his running mate on the back end of our defense, played a significant role in his success. As quiet as Polamalu could be, Clark loved to talk and he was good at it. It's no surprise that someone so articulate and knowledgeable about football has become a top NFL analyst for ESPN since retiring as a player.

Clark had an interesting story. He was totally the opposite of Polamalu in how he got to the Steelers. We did not draft him. No one did, which is why the NFL draft is such an inexact science. It's easy to look back, especially after the career that Clark had, and ask how a smart, tough player who had come out of a major program at LSU did not get drafted. A lot of that has to do with the pre-draft process.

They time them, have them lift weights and jump, and then the player gets stacked off those numbers. Those measurables really help, but they're not the determining factor as to who ends up winning the game. It's the guy who is productive and can perform when the pressure's on and can integrate information, the guy who can take it from the practice field, take it from the meeting room, and go out on the field and execute the game plan the way it was designed. These are the guys who are always in the right place at the right time. That was Clark. He was a sure tackler, and it didn't matter what his 40 time was because he never wasted a step. You've heard the saying: "He runs a 4.6, but he'll play 4.4." That's true. Or you can run 4.4 but play 4.7. Clark was the former and he was a great athlete even if he did not have top-end speed. He was a very, very smart and unselfish player.

He was also available after we won the 2005 Super Bowl. We lost Chris Hope in free agency, and Bill Cowher told me to find the best free safety in free agency. I came back with Clark. I said, "Coach, this is the guy who fits us the best. In talking to him, I just think he'll step right in and fit in with the team."

Probably the best asset that I had to give to the Steelers and anybody else I worked for was I had so much experience. I knew what I was looking at. Was I right 100 percent of the time? No, I sure wasn't. It's an inexact science, but I think I had as much on-the-job and practical experience in identifying who could play defensive back, linebacker, or defensive line as anybody in the league when I was coaching. That was my strong suit. I made mistakes, but I was right a lot of times, too.

Clark signed with the Steelers and he was one of the best free agents that I ever got. It was like Christmas, and under the tree was a great present because he and Polamalu teamed up to give us the best safety tandem in the league for a number of years.

Clark played well for us from the outset, but he went through the ultimate scare in Denver in 2007. Clark has sickle cell trait and during the game he experienced sharp pains that had nothing to do with football. The high altitude had triggered a catastrophic reaction, and Clark was rushed to the hospital. It was a touch-and-go thing there for a while. We were just hoping we'd get Clark back. We weren't worried about how much football he was going to play.

He eventually had his spleen and gall bladder removed and lost 30 pounds. He missed the rest of the season, but Clark was nothing if not fearless. He returned in 2008, and that is when he and Polamalu really came into their own playing off one another, like they were joined at the hip. I watched them for years, and there was no verbal communication. Polamalu would look at Clark, and Clark would look back at Polamalu. Somehow, he would convey to Clark what he was going to do on that play. I still think it was more telepathic. I never could hear them say anything and I watched them pretty closely.

Polamalu was right so many times and made so many explosive plays. If he did make a mistake, Clark was always sitting right there to make the tackle or bat the pass down. Nothing better illustrated how cohesive the whole defense was than their symbiosis, and we had some pretty darn good cornerbacks with them in the secondary. We had three starting-caliber ones in Ike Taylor, Deshea Townsend, and Bryant McFadden and the luxury of five pretty good cornerbacks. We would need all of them—and some outside help during the season—because of injuries in our defensive backfield.

Taylor was more of a character than I ever realized. The thing as a coach that you liked most about him was he wasn't afraid of anybody or any assignment. He was a competitor and accepted any challenge you put on him. If he had a couple of plays he didn't like, he couldn't wait to get back out on the field. What more can you ask for from an athlete?

You just wanted to put your arms around him because he would come in every day, every week, and he'd say, "Coach, just tell me who I got this week and turn me loose." He would take the opponent's best receiver every week. He never complained and never had an excuse. He just went out there and competed.

Taylor had bounced back from a tough 2006 season. He got benched for a stretch, but I was confident he would be okay in the long run. We worked on little stuff after that season, mostly defensive backfield drills and a lot of ball drills. Most of it was checking off his fundamentals and making sure that he was still doing the things that he had been doing when he was really playing productively and being successful.

You're not going to play corner and come through a season and say, "I played great every game." It just doesn't happen at that position, kind of like at quarterback. Taylor was a great cover guy, a physical player. He could have been a better interceptor of the ball, but he usually kept the other guy from catching it. And he was not going to get rattled if the other guy made a play or two. If you're playing against a great quarterback and a great receiver, they're going to catch the ball; I don't care who you are. That's the position.

There were not a lot of passing yards—or offense—in the second game of the season at Cleveland. Weather helped dictate a defensive contest. Lake Erie can make Municipal Stadium feel like the coldest place in the world, especially at night. The wind coming off the lake was gusting at 40 miles an hour, even though it was the middle of September. That and some rain were from remnants of Hurricane Ike (not Taylor) as it passed up the East Coast.

We gained 281 total yards, and the Cleveland Browns gained 208. At halftime we had 108, and they had 97. It was that kind of game. The whole first quarter, Cleveland couldn't get out of the shadow of its own end zone. The Browns made only one first down, and we kept pinning them in their own territory. Their six possessions in the first half went like this: punt, punt, punt, punt, interception, interception.

The first interception came on their first play of the second quarter, and it was a deep ball. McFadden, who started in place of the injured Townsend, intercepted it. That was a pleasant sight to see: our depth showing up with players stepping up into the starting role and producing.

After that pick our offense drove 70 yards, culminating with Ben Roethlisberger's 10-yard touchdown pass to Hines Ward. We didn't know it at the time, but that was all the points we were going to need.

Cleveland mounted a 14-play drive late in the first half and got down to our 11-yard line. I was hoping to hold the Browns to three points. Polamalu had other ideas. On a pass play, he sat down, read the quarterback, and broke quickly. He made the interception to get us out of the half with a 7–0 lead. Polamalu made a great play, which is to say it was Troy being Troy.

We got the first points of the second half on a very impressive 48-yard field goal by Jeff Reed. A 48-yard pass from Roethlisberger to Santonio Holmes set up our final score of the game, which was just enough on this miserable weather night.

Cleveland mounted two more lengthy drives, and twice we held the Browns to field goals. The second one came in the fourth quarter when we were protecting a 10–3 lead. It was a 60-yard drive, and the Browns got down to our 20-yard line with three-and-a-half minutes left in the game. LaMarr Woodley and Larry Foote stopped this drive with two excellent plays. They both beat blockers on running plays that put the Browns into a third-down passing situation, and McFadden knocked down the pass. Cleveland kicked the field goal to cut the lead to 10–6. That ended up as the final score.

The offense ran all but 26 seconds off the three-and-a-half minutes left in the game. Roethlisberger was famous for that. He could eat the fourth quarter clock up like nobody. When we had Jerome Bettis and Roethlisberger in 2004–05, you did not want to get behind the Steelers in the fourth quarter. Defensive end Aaron Smith snuffed out whatever faint hopes Cleveland had of coming back when it got the ball back with 26 seconds left in the game. He sacked quarterback Derek Anderson, securing a 10–6 win that was not beautiful but moved us to 2–0. Smith had both of our sacks, something that is not easy to do for a defensive end in a 3-4 defense like ours. But by then I was never surprised by what he did on the field. He was that good of a player.

From One Shutdown Cornerback to Another

Dick LeBeau played 14 seasons with the Detroit Lions, teaming with Hall of Famers Dick "Night Train" Lane, Yale Lary, and Lem Barney to form a secondary that was one of the most feared in the NFL. LeBeau is widely considered to be one of the greatest defensive backs in Lions history. His 62 career interceptions are still a Lions record.

Bryant McFadden learned about LeBeau as a player after the Pittsburgh Steelers selected the Florida State cornerback in the second round of the 2005 NFL Draft. "I did my research and I'm like, 'Man, Coach LeBeau was a baller. This man was a beast,'" McFadden said. "So I was a fan before I actually met him."

For those who did not do their...ahem...research, LeBeau was always more than happy to give an oral history lesson. "He'd walk by us and look at all the players and be like, 'Five, seven, 12, 15, 20,'" safety Troy Polamalu said. "We'd be like, 'What is he doing these numbers for?' And then he'd say, 'All of you guys don't equal the amount that I had.'"

LeBeau is loathe to talk about himself. So it was not braggadocio. It was more him having some fun with his players. It may have been a subtle form of gamesmanship with players on a defense that was filled with what linebacker Larry Foote called "competitive junkies."

LeBeau's career interceptions total is still tied for 10th in NFL history. "He reminded us daily," cornerback Deshea Townsend said.

Ike Taylor has a similar memory. "I remember him walking by, and he would say, 'How many interceptions do you have in your career, Ike Taylor?' I would say however many, and he would ask Troy Polamalu. He would ask everybody how many interceptions did we have. We'd give a number and we would be way short of his total. He'd say, 'You all got 30 or 40 more to go.' I'll never forget him telling us how many we had to get to catch him."

Taylor is nothing if not a character. Perhaps it is fitting then that he refers to LeBeau as "Dicky," the name "Night Train" Lane, another character, called LeBeau when the two played cornerback for the Lions from 1960 to 1965.

Taylor may not have quite played it at the Pro Football Hall of Fame level as Lane did, but he won two Super Bowls with the Steelers and enjoyed a successful career. One of the reasons why the Steelers had a defense for the ages in 2008: LeBeau never lost any sleep knowing that Taylor would shadow top-flight receivers week in and week out. "It was amazing how many times he would shut his guy out or hold him to very few catches," LeBeau said. "He was the guy who really let us be a constant pressure team. You couldn't run the zone blitz without setting it up with max blitz, and Ike was the guy that enabled us to do that because I never felt we were going to be in trouble one-on-one with him on the best receiver anybody had."

That is the definition of a shutdown cornerback. "Man, that's all I wanted," Taylor said. "People want to know what a shutdown corner is. It is: 'You got him, you got the team's best receiver. Wherever he goes, you go every snap'. Obviously, I did well enough for my coaching staff and LeBeau to say, 'Every time we line up against a team, Ike's playing this team's best receiver.'"

Taylor took a circuitous path to becoming a No. 1 cornerback and a cornerstone on Steelers defenses for more than a decade. He played college football for only two seasons after walking on at Louisiana-Lafayette as a junior. After playing running back, he moved to cornerback his senior season and played well enough there for the Steelers to take the 6'2", 195 pounder in the fourth round of the 2003 NFL Draft.

Taylor played all 16 games as a rookie in a reserve role and also returned kickoffs. The next year, LeBeau returned to Pittsburgh for a second stint as defensive coordinator, and Taylor quickly caught his eye. "When I got on the field with him, I saw that he was a special athlete, and he had size and strength and speed," said LeBeau, who played cornerback for 14 NFL seasons. "I could usually find some techniques that would help young defensive backs. Mostly, it was teaching him angles and how to use his hands, and he did the rest."

Taylor played 12 NFL seasons—all with the Steelers. Most of those, he was clearly the team's top cornerback. "He was wonderful to coach. I never had a cross word with Ike," LeBeau said. "Never had him say anything much more than, 'Who do I have this week, Coach?' He was a great player."

—G.V.B.

3

Not-So Brotherly Love in Philly

In 2005 things didn't look real promising after an early December loss to the Cincinnati Bengals at Heinz Field. It dropped our record to 7–5 and left little to no margin for error just for us to make the playoffs. We had dealt with some injuries and lost three straight games, but we were better than our record indicated.

We showed it the next week on a wintry day at Heinz Field. We beat the Chicago Bears 21–9 and really imposed our will on them. Nothing exemplified our physical dominance that day more than when Jerome Bettis trucked Brian Urlacher as snow fell from the skies. Both were terrific players, future Pro Football Hall of Famers, and Bettis just happened to get the better of him on that play. The win started the run that did not end until two months later when we won the Super Bowl in Detroit, Bettis' hometown.

It also produced my favorite Aaron Smith story.

Fire-zone blitzes were a staple of our defense and required our two inside linebackers to cross or loop around each other before blitzing up the middle. Defensive linemen, who are usually rushing the quarterback or kicking the crap out of an offensive lineman, had to peel off on fire-zone blitzes and take somebody leaving the backfield or a tight end and run with him. Before I called one of those blitzes, Smith and I were talking on the sidelines. He said, "Now what if this guy just takes off at the snap and he don't give a damn who's blitzing or not?"

I said, "Well, you just take off with him." He looked at me, and I said, "Look, don't worry. Ike is trapping in behind you, and if he's running away from you, Ike will be sitting right back there to get him."

The offense was moving the ball a little bit, and I called the zone blitz that had Ike Taylor trapping, which meant showing man-to-man coverage but playing a short zone, and Smith was peeling. Well, shoot, Thomas Jones of the Chicago Bears caught a pass, ran away from Smith, and Smith was running his ass off. Taylor missed his check and didn't show up where he was supposed to be. Jones caught the ball, and Smith was probably five yards behind him and just running as fast as he could run. It made it look like Jones just flat-out beat Smith. The Bears made about 20 yards on the play.

Before I had a chance to get to Smith after he came off the field, he stomped over to me and said, "You told me Ike was going to be there! You told me I wouldn't be alone!"

He was so mad, and I didn't know what he was going to do, but he was coming right for me. I said, "Well, he'll be there the next time when we run it again. Just relax." He was upset with the ol' coach.

Smith was one of the greatest competitors I've ever seen. He was also one of the best players I ever coached. He had come to the Pittsburgh Steelers from Northern Colorado, a small school and hardly a football factory. He had been an outstanding young basketball player, which testifies to his athleticism. He was not a particularly big guy coming out of college, but he knew what he wanted to do with his life in terms of competing, and that was to play in the NFL.

He worked, trained, and dieted and he became a very strong, smart, athletic defensive end. I would say over the course of the season you might see him blocked an average of one time a game. You couldn't block the guy. If you started with an advantage before the play was over, he was going to fight, claw, and get his tail where he was supposed to be and get his end of it done. The whole defense had that attitude. He knew his position and he had such personal pride in his own performance and he was a wonderful teammate. But he was his own toughest critic and did not ever want to lose one play. He very seldom did.

I was not with the Pittsburgh Steelers when they drafted Smith or Brett Keisel, our other starting defensive end. There were a lot of similarities between the two. Keisel, like Smith, was an athletic guy who had excelled in basketball. He could have played it at a Division I school had he chosen to take that path. Also like Smith, Keisel wasn't real big coming out of college.

He had been taken by the Steelers with the second of their two seventh-round picks in the 2002 NFL Draft. The 242nd selection of that draft fought his way onto the team—and stayed there—with his special teams play. In 2003 before I returned to Pittsburgh, he missed the entire year because of a shoulder injury. Before I ever saw him on the field, he showed me something by just how he battled back from that.

Keisel, a rangy, athletic end, became a part of the defensive line rotation in 2005. The next year he moved into the starting lineup. He started all 16 games and recorded five-and-a-half sacks. Frustration, though, set in the following season. Keisel felt miscast in a defense in which the defensive ends' primary responsibility was occupying blockers to free up linebackers. He thought he could do more.

So one morning he took me up on my open-door policy. He was sitting in my office when I walked in. I said, "What's up, big boy! How are you doing?"

"Not too good," Keisel said.

He told me that he thought he could do more than just tie up blockers. He did not stop there. He asked how he was ever going to make a Pro Bowl, get a big contract if he was not also rushing the passer and dropping into coverage.

I explained how well our defense had ranked statistically as a whole. "Let me get something through your thick head. I make decisions on our defense for us to be No. 1, for us to be the best defense as a whole that we can be," I said. "If you think I'm making decisions for James [Harrison] or Troy or other guys to make all the plays and to be All-Pro, you're a fool. You are a great guy up front. You force people to take two guys to block you. That's a weapon. Maybe you don't want to be that weapon anymore. Maybe I should find someone else to do this job."

Keisel was mortified after we finished our chat. "Coach, I can't wait to practice double teams at practice today," he said. "Please! I love being on this defense."

And he showed how dedicated he was. When I would come into work, which was reasonably early in the morning, Keisel was already in the building and in the weight room. I made a little mental note that he probably was going to end up being a pretty good football player. He was that dedicated. Keisel and Smith both made themselves into great players.

Any discussion of great players on that defense has to include a lengthy one on Casey Hampton, one of my favorite players. When you talk about a prototypical nose tackle, you would make the exact dimensions and demeanor of Hampton. He was, in my opinion, the best interior lineman in the league when he played. No one talked about Hampton too much, but if you are going to play an odd-man front, you need a great nose tackle if you're going to be great, and, boy, was he great.

You couldn't block him in part because he moved so well for his size. Centers got so worried about him that they would start cheating to try to beat him to a spot. I came up with a technique, and we called it "Tough." Larry Foote and James Farrior would cover for him by flying to the other side of the flow of the ball, so Hampton could go right behind the center who overcompensated to try to keep Hampton from ruining the play. In "Tough" Hampton could just swat the center and go backdoor, knowing the linebackers were adjusting behind him. I'd tell Hampton, "Now whenever you think it's time for 'Tough,' when you think the center is running on you, just let me know."

I'd be on the sidelines, walking and thinking, and Hampton would walk by. He wouldn't pause. He wouldn't stop. He would just say, "Time for a little 'Tough,' Coach."

I would turn him loose on the backside. He had a better feel for when it was time to use it than I did because he was right there at the nose. The two fronts fit his talents and his abilities perfectly. If you were too slow when he was across from you, he would beat you to the spot. If you were running to cut him off, he'd go the backside.

You have to be unselfish to play nose tackle in a three-man set because you're not going to get sacks. Hampton never complained about it. He just did his part and anchored the whole defense. Everything revolved around him being able to get his part done. If you get the center inverted, teams are not going to be able to run the ball. The odds were very good that Hampton was going to be able to invert the center on 90 percent of the snaps. Inverting recreates the line of scrimmage because when the ball's snapped the center is pushed into the backfield. It takes away the room that the running back has of cutting and finding the hole.

What I love about Hampton is that what you see is what you're getting. He is himself 1,000 percent of the time. All he did was do his job and he was so damn good at what he did that I think he expected everybody else to be that good. That wasn't going to happen, and every now and then, he'd look funny at a defensive back or someone if they made a space error.

One thing I preached from Day One was nobody critiqued any other player but me. Every now and again, I would have to say, "Now, Casey, get your hands off your hips and get in the huddle and get your part of it. Don't be coaching the defensive backs." He, though, was a nearly ideal player to coach. He didn't say anything, didn't ask anything, just played.

Our defense had played well in the first two games of the season and had yet to give up a touchdown when the game was still in question. The Houston Texans scored both of their touchdowns in the season opener after we had opened a 38–3 lead, and we had held the Cleveland Browns to just two field goals.

We faced a multi-faceted challenge in the third week of the season, starting with history. The Steelers had not won in Philadelphia since 1965 when the Eagles were playing in Franklin Field. I had played there, so it had been a few years. The City of Brotherly Love had been anything but that to the Steelers, who had lost eight straight times in Philadelphia.

This time we were going up against a head coach who is always a very formidable offensive mind in head coach Andy Reid, and he did not lack material with which to work. Donovan McNabb was a darn good quarterback, and Brian Westbrook was a top-notch, all-purpose back. He could score rushing or receiving. DeSean Jackson had really burst onto the scene as a rookie wide receiver. He could flat out fly. He had caught passes of 62 and 48 yards in the Eagles' first two games, and that big-play ability had certainly caught our attention. We rolled coverages at him some to give him problems with releases off the line of scrimmage and getting separation downfield.

It quickly became apparent that Philadelphia's game plan was to throw quickly, somewhat negating Jackson's impact. Most people tried to attack us that way: run the ball—well, try to anyway—and get rid of it quick because of our pass rush. We had five great linebackers with LaMarr Woodley, James Harrison, Farrior, Foote, and Lawrence Timmons, who was getting a lot of playing time and was a hell of a pass rusher. They were all fast and quick, so teams really didn't want to mess with us, particularly in long-yardage situations because we were going to disguise things.

McNabb came out throwing quick and he was very accurate and in rhythm. On third and 17, McNabb completed a 19-yard in route to Jason Avant at our 25-yard line. We rarely gave up first downs when the situation was tilted so heavily in our favor. But it was a hell of a throw and a catch. Our defense quickly bounced back. McNabb completed a five-yard pass to running back Tony Hunt, but a bunch of our guys broke on the ball and whacked him. He fumbled the ball, and Bryant McFadden, who was starting again for the injured Deshea Townsend, recovered it. He was ruled down before the ball came out, but our guys upstairs got a good look at the play and told Mike Tomlin to challenge it. The call was overturned. So it was a big play for us to get off the field after they had moved the ball.

Our guys answered with a really nice drive of their own. We picked up four first downs as Ben Roethlisberger hit some quick hitch passes and 16-yard completions to Santonio Holmes and Nate Washington. The drive stalled at the Eagles' 19-yard line, and Jeff Reed kicked a field goal near the end of the first quarter. It was our first lead of the game. Unfortunately, it would prove to be our only lead of the game.

Philadelphia responded with another good drive, mixing the run with quick passes. On third and 15, McNabb threw deep left to Hank Baskett for 20 yards and a first down. On third and 3, we had another chance to get off the field, but McNabb completed a three-yard pass to running back Lorenzo Booker for a first down on our 20-yard line.

Another Eagles running back burned us on the next play. Correll Buckhalter, who had six catches in the game, caught a short pass in the flat. He got to the boundary and scored on the damn thing for the only touchdown of the game. That capped a 13-play, 86-yard drive, and Philadelphia added a field goal after recovering a fumble on our 45-yard line.

The game could have started slipping away after Philadelphia intercepted a deep Roethlisberger pass on our next possession, but the defense came through when we really needed it. With a little less than two minutes left in the first half, McFadden intercepted a third-down pass on the Philadelphia 49-yard line. Timmons came clean on the back end and hit McNabb just as he was throwing. McNabb bruised his chest, and it resulted in a fluttering ball. It was our second takeaway of the half, and we needed both. McNabb had gone 112 passes without an interception before that play. Reed nailed a 53-yard field goal to make the score 10–6.

I told our guys at halftime that we had to play better. It was going to be a low-scoring, one-play game, and we had to get the ball back quicker for our offense to give them more opportunities. I thought we were just a step behind in a lot of things. Whenever we were having trouble, the first thing I did was simplify things, not call anything where everybody had to read very much. Just take off and go. I think it helped us get going because we looked like ourselves defensively in the second half. I wish I had started that a little bit sooner because the Eagles had moved the ball their first two possessions.

I figured Philadelphia's defense would play well against us. They had given up 41 points the week before in a close loss to the Dallas Cowboys and they were just too good to struggle two games in a row. Eagles defensive coordinator Jim Johnson was an excellent coach and had the personnel to execute his attacking defense. The Eagles played all game like a talented defense that was still smarting from giving up 41 points to a hated rival the previous game. They sacked Roethlisberger nine times and held Willie Parker to 20 rushing yards on 13 carries. We converted just 2-of-13 third downs.

Yet, it was still anybody's game deep into the fourth quarter. We were still down only 10–6 when an under-siege Roethlisberger got called for intentional grounding in the end zone. That gave the Eagles a safety, and we weren't able to recover in a 15–6 loss.

Even though I was not happy with how we started, we still forced three turnovers—one of them a third-quarter interception by Troy Polamalu that helped keep us in the game. The ball got tipped, and Polamalu, like he was shot out like a cannon, dove, and got his hands under the ball. It was one of those plays where only he could have done that.

We were just as physical as the Eagles. We held them to 260 yards of total offense, and McNabb missed the first series of the third quarter after taking that shot in the ribs. Westbrook got knocked out early with injury after he had managed just 12 rushing yards on five carries.

We left Philadelphia with a 2–1 record but had to quickly turn the page. The Baltimore Ravens were coming to Pittsburgh for a *Monday*

Night Football showdown. As with most Steelers–Ravens games during this era, the *MNF* broadcast should have come with a parental viewing warning. The next installment of this great rivalry would indeed be that violent.

The Anchor

Casey Hampton defied convention and not just because he moved so well for a man whom the Pittsburgh Steelers generously listed at 325 pounds. As tough as he was on the field—Hampton set the standard for 3-4 nose tackles during a Steelers career in which he made five Pro Bowls and probably had a case to go every year—he had a tender side off it and was one of the most popular players in the locker room. Geography reflected that.

Hampton's locker was next to kicker Jeff Reed's with other specialists nearby. He looked out of place but fit right in because of his utter lack of pretense and hearty laugh that seemed to emanate from his belly. "Hamp was the most fun guy, and everyone seemed to talk to him," defensive end Brett Keisel said. "He was cool with everyone. He was just a special, special guy."

"Hamp was kind of a jokester," defensive end Aaron Smith said, "that guy who is a fun-loving kid that everybody enjoyed."

Not everybody enjoyed him.

The Steelers consistently were at or near the top of the NFL in rushing defense when Hampton manned the middle of it. That played right into what defensive coordinator Dick LeBeau wanted to do: make offenses one-dimensional. It started with Hampton. His unique blend of strength, agility, and quickness made him a constant mismatch. "It was mind-boggling to see him move and watch him take on three guys all at the point of attack," Keisel said, "He was definitely our anchor. We wouldn't have had that ability to really take people's run games and throw it in the fire and be able to unleash blitzes and get after the quarterback."

Another thing that made Hampton so valuable is that he was built for the back-alley brawls that defined Baltimore Ravens–Steelers games during his era. There was no subtlety when the AFC North rivals met on the field. It was power versus power. And strength versus strength since the two teams were so similar—from roster construction to the mindset of their players. "Defensively, we felt like we were the bullies, and their defense felt like they were the bullies, and that's just how it went down," Hampton said. "We tried to bully each other. Whoever runs the ball the best is going to win. We felt like had to go out there and prove every time that we had a better defense. I just never understood why we never got the credit some other teams got. I thought we were head and shoulders above those guys."

—S.B.

4

Blitzing Baltimore

I COACHED 45 YEARS IN THE NFL AFTER STARTING AS A SPECIAL TEAMS coach with the Philadelphia Eagles. I am best remembered as a defensive coordinator and for my role in the birth of the zone blitz. People ask me how I came up with that, and the short answer is that I played 14 seasons in the NFL and during that time I soaked up everything I could.

I studied film the whole time I was around football. When I got done with practice as an NFL player, I'd go watch the guys I was playing against that week. I also watched people I thought were pretty good defensive backs and watched different schemes of defense. I was a football junkie. Once I figured out what to look for, I became intrigued by why some things worked better than others. I had ideas as a player, and my philosophy on bringing pressure was shaped by my playing days.

When I first came into the league in 1959, everybody played a 4-3 defense. It was mostly zone with only a little bit of man-to-man or zero blitz. After the NFL-AFL merger in 1970, people started playing 11 up—something we were already doing—and bump-and-run coverage by the cornerbacks with the other nine up at the ball.

Jim David was a longtime cornerback for the Detroit Lions who became our defensive coordinator during this time. On the day we put in the game plan, he would fill every square on the blackboard, which dominated our meeting room, with a blitz on it. I loved it, even though it put a lot on cornerbacks since we often had to play man-to-man coverage with no safety help.

I retired from playing after the 1972 season and immediately went into coaching. By the time I joined Green Bay Packers coach Bart Starr's staff in 1976 as a defensive backs coach, a significant shift had occurred. Teams had pretty much caught up with the zero blitz and started using option routes. If a guy blitzed, the wide receiver would break his route off, and the quarterback would hit him right away. Offenses had the answers, so

I started working on the look of an all-out blitz. Instead of sending six or seven players, I would only send five and then steal a lineman from the other side of the blitz to play an underneath area. This was the foundation of the zone blitz, marrying pressure on the ball with a fail-safe player somewhere, but it was still only a theory, still only on paper.

I might have never had a chance to try it if not for Sam Wyche. He became the Cincinnati Bengals' head coach in 1984. I had been Cincinnati's defensive backs coach the previous four seasons, and Wyche promoted me to defensive coordinator. By then I had worked on the zone blitz enough—again, in theory—that I thought I could do something with it. Fortunately for me, Wyche was a very innovative coach. He was one of the first coaches to use the no-huddle offense and would try anything. If I would have gone to most head coaches as the defensive coordinator and said, "I want to blitz two little guys and drop a big guy," they probably would have looked at me like I was crazy.

Instead, Wyche said, "Yeah, let's take a look at it."

Another coach I need to mention is Bill Arnsparger, who had been Don Shula's defensive coordinator when the Miami Dolphins won two Super Bowls in the early 1970s with the famed "Killer Bs" defenses. Arnsparger had done a couple of things when it came to dropping guys into coverage and he was the athletic director at the University of Florida in the mid-1980s when I went there to work out some players before the NFL draft.

I knew he had an Ohio background and I stopped in his office before leaving Gainesville, Florida. I told him I admired his career and that I really liked some of the things he had done disguising blitzes. He said, "Well, Dick, I was just looking for a safer way to blitz." I had a flight to Los Angeles, and my plane was taking off in an hour and 15 minutes. As I drove to the airport. I said to myself, *That's exactly what I want.*

I started drawing up defenses on that flight, which was four hours. By the time we got on the ground, I had some stuff I could look at when I got back to my job as defensive coordinator. One of the ways of getting pressure was bringing safeties. That meant that whoever the safety was supposed to cover in a man blitz had to be covered by somebody else—usually the other safety or a slot cornerback. Those players often had a near-impossible job. They had to cover for a blitzing player without revealing their intentions before the snap. Whoever was supposed to go pick up coverage for the blitzing safety couldn't get there in time. My train of thought was, *Well, what if when they break away from the guy who's coming to get them, we trapped that area with a zone player and went over the top with another zone player?*

All I wanted to do was put a little crimp in their plan, especially the West Coast offense that Bill Walsh and the San Francisco 49ers had popularized. That's kind of the history of any sport. The offense does something, and then the defense figures out a way to address it. What evolved from that is people who don't normally blitz were blitzing all over the place and people who very seldom did anything other but play the three-point stance were dropping off to take areas or pick up a back out of the backfield. You were breaking the rules of pass protection for the offense.

The first time we ran a fire-zone in a preseason game, the tight end broke off his route, and my trap zone cornerback picked off the pass and ran it back 45 yards for a touchdown. That was an epiphany for me. Were there some moments where the swimming pool was empty, and I hit the concrete? Yeah, but I kept hammering it out, and whenever you're doing something that no one's done, you have to create a package that you can teach it from. We came up with a set of rules that with a bit of experience held up game in and game out. I had a head start on everybody because we were the only ones doing it originally. So we went through a lot of the *snakes*—we used to use the term *snakes* as something that the offenses can do that can really hurt defenses on zone blitzes—and I had eliminated a lot of those on the practice field before we ever took it into a game.

A seminal moment for me came in 1987. We were playing the Dolphins and star quarterback Dan Marino in Cincinnati. By then Marino was well on his way to becoming a first-ballot Pro Football Hall of Famer, but this was the first time we were playing against him with the zone blitz. We had a hell of a quarterback in our own right in Boomer Esiason and we played the Dolphins tough before losing 20–14. Boomer and Marino were buddies, and after the game, Boomer told me, "Hey, I was talking to Marino, and he said, 'What the hell was the shit they were doing? After half a quarter, I stopped looking at my pre-snap keys and just started looking at my man and throwing to lead him open and I didn't look at nothing else.'"

That was definitely a eureka moment for me because what you're trying to do as a defensive coach is make the quarterback read everything *after* the ball is snapped. If he knows where you're going defensively before the ball is snapped in the National Football League, you're going to have a long, long night. I thought, *Man, if I can make a quarterback say, "All I'm going to do is look at my guy," then I'm heading in the right direction because that means he can't read all the other guys and where they're going.*

One defining trait of the 2008 Pittsburgh Steelers defense was the players were so smart and so dialed in during the week that I did not have to worry too much about overloading them. We had probably 50 different blitzes, and there's no way you can practice that many. You scripted 40 plays in practice and you could only run a blitz every few plays. I probably had as many blitzes as anybody who had ever coached and I walked the players through them practically every day since I couldn't run them in practice because there were so many of them.

We wanted to have pressures that were effective versus all phases of any formation. If you got in a game—and you often did—where a team was running formations and plays that you really hadn't seen them run in the previous games, then you didn't have to throw your hands up in the air and say, "I don't know what to call." I would look at what was hurting us. Is the ball going to the closed side or to the open side? To the left side or the right side? Up the middle? Unbalanced? We could pressure whatever formation we were getting that was giving us a problem.

I didn't like to get one particular pattern of blitzing on video too many times. If a certain pattern of blitz had shown up a significant amount of times in the game we just played, I would change it the next week. That way, the opponent wasn't going to see all the tendencies and looks that thcy would bc practicing against.

Most of that was common sense from experience. In terms of making a game plan, you planned around who their best players were, what you had seen them do in previous games, and then you prepared for that. Every good general has a good Plan A, B, C, and maybe D because what happens if Plan A doesn't work? That was the way I prepared our guys every week. I preached that the offenses get to go into the huddle and call their play knowing who's carrying the ball, who's throwing the ball, who's catching the ball, and what the ball is going to be snapped on. The defense knows none of that. We only know where the ball is and, after they get out of the huddle, we know what formation they're in after they get done shifting and motioning.

I always tried to even that up a little bit by giving the other guy something to think about. We were going to be moving. We were not going to be where we lined up originally at the snap and we were going to be blitzing. A defense that moves around a lot before the snap and has so many different blitzes can give young quarterbacks trouble, especially rookies. We were facing one of those in the fourth week of the season, but we knew that game might be as tough as any we had played in the first month of the season.

It was Baltimore week, and that means something in Pittsburgh. Almost all our games against the Baltimore Ravens from that era were close, hard-fought battles. Both teams were built on defense, so they were reasonably low-scoring games usually decided by seven points and quite often by three points.

Coming off our first loss, I saw this as a challenge game. How were we going to handle that adversity? This Monday night game at Heinz Field turned into a test of our mettle in a lot of different ways. We went into it without Casey Hampton and Brett Keisel, who were out with injuries. Early in the third quarter Chris Hoke, who was filling in for Hampton and was also an excellent nose tackle, went down with an injury. By that time we were down to our third nose tackle in Orpheus Roye, a solid veteran. We also trailed 13–3.

The Ravens had controlled the second quarter, and a late touchdown set up by a big pass play from Joe Flacco, their rookie quarterback, and Derrick Mason gave them a 10-point lead at halftime. We needed to come out of halftime and establish some positive football. There were four punts to start the third quarter. Then a plodding game suddenly changed after Ben Roethlisberger hit Santonio Holmes for a 38-yard touchdown. On the very next series James Harrison sacked Flacco. LaMarr Woodley scooped up the loose ball and scored, giving us 14 points in 15 seconds and a 17–13 lead. A Woodley sack forced a three-and-out, and we were really rolling. Roethlisberger hit Hines Ward with a 49-yard pass, but we were not able to punch in what might have been a game-sealing touchdown. Jeff Reed's chip-shot field goal made it 20–13 with nine minutes left in the game.

Baltimore refused to go away. Flacco hit a couple of passes, and Mason, who had a good night, set up the game-tying touchdown with a catch with four minutes left to play. The game went into overtime, and Baltimore got the ball first after winning the coin toss. Our coverage team did a great job of keeping Baltimore plugged up, and there was also a facemask penalty on that kickoff putting the ball on the Ravens' 15-yard line. This was our chance defensively.

Throughout the year our special teams' good kicking and coverage kept the opponent backed up, which really helped our defense. I think that was another positive aspect of this season. We had strong special teams play all year long, and that unit made a play at put-up-or-shut-up time that contributed to this win.

On third and 15, I called an inside fire-zone. Lawrence Timmons got free after a perfectly executed loop and sacked Flacco. That forced Baltimore to punt from deep in its own territory, giving us the advantage in field position. After the punt we only needed a couple of first downs to get into field-goal range. On third and 8 near midfield, Roethlisberger hit a 24-yard pass to Mewelde Moore, which went down to the Ravens' 31-yard line. The more demanding the situation, the more productive Roethlisberger was usually going to be. This was just another case in point. Our receivers were clutch, too. If you put the ball in their vicinity, they were going to come down with it. We ran the ball two times, and Roethlisberger hit a little check-down pass, setting up Reed's game-winning 46-yard field goal. That was a very hard-fought victory and a very critical one for us coming off our first loss and playing defense without three of our starting linemen—two for the whole game.

We held the Ravens to 3.1 yards per carry, and they tried to run on us because of the injuries but had only 243 yards of total offense. We sacked Flacco five times, another impressive statistic given our injuries up front. The defensive line has to execute a lot of the variables of the fire-zone defense for it to be effective because guys who don't normally rush are rushing, and people who don't normally drop in pass coverage are dropping. All those guys, who played because of injuries, had to be able to execute that part of it and do it at a level where we could still win the game. They executed that well, indicating that this team was going to have depth to withstand injuries at different positions.

Beating Baltimore was always crucial for us, and the game was typical of Pittsburgh–Baltimore games of that era. They almost always came down to a couple of plays. We had made enough of them to improve to 3–1 at the quarter point of the season. Next up was a road game against an opponent that always seemed to give us fits.

An Infamous Wardrobe Malfunction

Football can be a funny game. That explains how Dick LeBeau ended up in *MAD* magazine after an equipment mishap during his playing days. While playing against the Dallas Cowboys, LeBeau ripped out the seat of his pants on a first down. He had to remain on the field for two more downs because of NFL rules at the time regarding substitutions. "I got a cleat in my butt, and they had those knit pants and they held your pants nice and tight, but if they got a snag, it just ripped," LeBeau said. "In those days an equipment replacement cost you a timeout, so you couldn't get anything fixed. I said to one of the refs, 'Look at my pants.' He said, 'Do you want an equipment timeout?' I said, 'Can I get one and not have it cost us a timeout?' He said, 'No, you can't.' I said, 'Hell, I ain't taking no timeout. I can play. My butt is hanging out. If you don't care, I guess I don't.'"

LeBeau compensated by holding a piece of elastic over his buttocks while the offenses and defense were huddling. Once they lined up, he dropped one drawer—so to speak—and played.

Fortunately for LeBeau, the Lions forced a punt after two more plays. LeBeau got to the sidelines after the punt return and alerted the team equipment manager to his predicament. "He got a needle—it looked like one of those needles my mom used to sew up the turkey at Thanksgiving—and a shoelace," LeBeau said, "and he stitches it up real quick and says, 'That will hold it.' We go back out on the field, and the first snap, there goes my butt hanging out again. So I've got to go another series holding on to these pants until they snap the ball."

When LeBeau returned to the sidelines, the equipment manager had a new pair of pants for him. The only thing was LeBeau had to change into them without the benefit of privacy. The equipment manager and a couple of staffers held up a couple of blankets as LeBeau changed but that only provided so much...ahem...coverage. "After you get 10 rows up, everybody in the stadium is looking at me standing there in my jockstrap changing," LeBeau said with a laugh. "We got the pants on and stuffed the pads in, and it was time for the defense to go back onto the field. I run onto the field and the thigh pads in football pants are cut around the groin area so that you don't have pads running up and pinching you where you don't want to be pinched. They put the pads in backward—my left pad on my right and my right pad on my left—so if I get hit down there in any kind of way, it's just going to mash my private parts. We get them stopped again, and I have to pull my pants down, so I can get the pads turned around. That was the saga of that story."

But the story was far from over. A picture of LeBeau holding up his pants while on the field found its way into *MAD* magazine. It ran inside the front cover with the caption, "Watch the 44. He plays rough." The joke turned out to be on the satire magazine in one respect. Beulah LeBeau *loved* the picture. "When my mom saw that, she got an 8 ½ x 11 frame and hung it over her bed for 30 years," LeBeau said. "My mom just thought that was a great picture: her son holding his pants up right in the middle of the game. When you're playing corner in the NFL, you ain't worried about one flap on your butt."

The postscript to the story provided what LeBeau interpreted as a sign from his mother, who passed away in October 2009 at the age of 96. In the spring of 2023, LeBeau looked through his mother's possessions for the photo but to no avail. On May 3 he received two pictures in the mail. They were from a man in Indiana who explained that he and his father collected sports memorabilia. He requested LeBeau's autograph on two of the *MAD* magazine pictures, which LeBeau had not seen in close to two decades.

What caused LeBeau to sit down: May 3rd is his mother's birthday. "It was surreal," he said. "I'm saying she sent it to me."

—G.V.B.

5

Ben Comes Up Big

It is amazing how much the NFL draft has grown from when I played and during my coaching career. It is now a three-day extravaganza with wall-to-wall TV coverage. Heck, more than 300,000 people attended the 2023 draft in Kansas City, Missouri.

There was such little fanfare surrounding the draft when the Cleveland Browns picked me out of Ohio State that I honestly cannot remember if I found out by phone or by letter. There were only 12 NFL teams then, and I was the 58th overall pick of the 1959 NFL Draft. My one liner is always: "I was drafted in today's second round" because today there are 64 guys drafted by the end of the second round. After I got drafted, I met one of the Browns coaches in a Columbus, Ohio, hotel room and received a $350 signing bonus. That was the most money I ever had in my life. I thought I was the richest guy on the planet.

Even when I started coaching in 1973, the draft was still just business. The scouts and the coaches all gathered in a hotel room, and teams had two representatives at the draft. We were hooked up by phone, and the reps would report how it's going on the draft floor. For example, they might say: "The Chicago Bears are on the clock. We're two picks away." It was not nearly as sophisticated and elaborate as what they do now.

The draft is huge for NFL teams, especially the Pittsburgh Steelers. They have had some legendary draft hauls since making a seminal pivot in the late 1960s when the draft became their primary tool for building their teams. When I returned to Pittsburgh for a second stint coaching in 2004, the Steelers were looking for a quarterback. If a coach ever asked me to evaluate an offensive prospect prior to the draft, I would do it and give him my opinion. But as a defensive coordinator, I had so many defensive players to watch on video, workouts to attend, and players to sort and put in some kind of order. In short, I largely focused on defense when preparing for a draft.

Ben Roethlisberger was an exception. In fact, the only offensive player I ever really stood on the table for was him. Living in Cincinnati until 2003, I was certainly aware of him in college. He played at Miami in Oxford, which is less than 40 miles from Cincinnati, and I was coaching the Cincinnati Bengals during his first two years of college. Even in 2003 after I had moved to Buffalo to be an assistant coach on Gregg Williams' Bills staff, I followed Roethlisberger. The Mid-American Conference had started playing on nights when its teams could get on national TV. Roethlisberger had a good team around him with skilled players, but none were NFL guys. It was amazing watching him, and I thought, *This guy is going to be a fantastic professional football player.*

What really sold me is when I watched Roethlisberger in the 2003 MAC Championship Game. The wind chill was like -8 degrees, and he was throwing the ball around like it was 78 in mid-July. He finished with 440 passing yards in his penultimate college game, and it was amazing the way he could handle himself.

I knew his coach, the late Terry Hoeppner, and I always thought Roethlisberger was unique with his size and his ability to play in weather that I thought would fit with us in Pittsburgh. We were drafting early enough in 2004 to maybe get a quarterback and we were looking for one. There were three top-notch passers in that draft—Philip Rivers, Eli Manning, and Roethlisberger. I spoke a couple of times and said, "I think Ben can't miss." When you hired me, I believed my opinion was what came along with it.

The last meeting before the draft had all the scouts and all the coaches. Bill Cowher said, "We're going to go through this one more time. I want to hear what everybody's going to say." He turned and looked at me and said, "Except you, LeBeau. I know how you feel."

I thought we were going to take Rivers, but he and Manning went in the first four picks. By the time we picked at No. 11, Roethlisberger was the only one left, which resolved it for us.

We went into the season with Roethlisberger as the backup quarterback and we won the first game. In the second game we were losing to the Ravens in Baltimore, and Tommy Maddox got hurt. Roethlisberger came in and played well under the circumstances in a 30–13 loss. Roethlisberger started the next week, and the rest is history. He set an NFL record by going 13–0 the rest of the season—he did not play in our final game since we had locked up home-field advantage in the AFC playoffs—and led us to the AFC Championship Game. You could just tell that the tighter the situation was, the more likely Roethlisberger was to come through. The next season he won a Super Bowl at the age of 23.

He was not the only star we had on offense in 2008. Like Roethlisberger, Hines Ward had been tremendous in that Super Bowl year of 2005. Ward is one of the greatest catchers of the ball that I've ever seen as well as probably the best blocking wide receiver. Given his durability and longevity and productivity, I don't think there's any question that he's a Pro Football Hall of Fame wide receiver. Think of all the great Steelers teams and great Steelers wide receivers, and Ward eclipsed all of their records.

I don't know what criteria you could come up with that he is not a Hall of Fame player—unless on-field popularity is one. Ward was one of those cocky guys and he was rough and tough. Half these rules they have now about cross blocking and coming back against the flow were put in there because of him. He was always looking to blow somebody up. Ward was not small—he was more than 200 pounds with good athleticism—and it didn't bother him to go over the middle. He was an aggressive competitor. He was a football player. With those kinds of guys, it's contagious and it rubs off on everybody. He was a pacesetter for us.

We had a game-breaker opposite him in Santonio Holmes, our 2006 first-round draft pick. He was a tremendous speed-and-route guy with great hands. Our tight end, Heath Miller, was also a fantastic asset for the offense. He and Roethlisberger seemed to have such chemistry. Whenever Roethlisberger was in trouble on third down and 8 in a crucial part of the game, he was going to get the ball anywhere near Miller, and Miller was going to catch it. There were a lot of pluses with the Steelers offense, but we lost All-Pro guard Alan Faneca to the New York Jets in free agency after the 2007 season. He is one of the best guards of his generation and is rightly in the Pro Football Hall of Fame. His loss was huge, and injuries during the season also created a lot of moving parts along the offensive line. The defense gave our team valuable time, in my mind, to settle in new personnel in the offense.

Bruce Arians, our offensive coordinator, was one of the better offensive coaches in the NFL. I think he established that in his subsequent record as a head coach. He's always been a productive coach, and you knew if you stayed around long enough, BA was going to figure out a way to get some points. It was always good to use training camp to sharpen yourself as a coordinator against an offensive coordinator like Arians. The most important thing when preparing for a season is keeping an eye on the big picture. Each side is going to have different objectives. Maybe two out of the three opponents in your division run no-huddle, and your offense may want to ground, pound, and huddle to shorten the game as much as possible.

Coaches have to be unselfish in that respect. I always requested to see as many different formations, different motions, different personnel as you could possibly get in a practice without diminishing its value to the offensive coaches. We were going to have to defend every single thing, and every week was going to be to a certain degree different. You had to be able to defend three tight ends on the field, a 300-pound fullback in the backfield, or a five-wide receiver set with nobody in the backfield. You were going to see all of that at some point and you were going to see it every game until you stopped it. You had to prepare players by seeing someone else do it against you. Then you could get your guys on the sidelines and show them what was happening and at least your thoughts on what would stop it. The only way you had a basis for them to relate was having practiced against it at some point and time. A lot of times, it would have been back in training camp where you have the most time to practice against everything. You had to synchronize because the offense was going to want to put in different packages.

I would script the first two weeks of training camp in the offseason. You might change a play here or there, but that had to be in lockstep with the offense. I didn't care if they passed every down or ran every down. I wanted to be able to face as many formations, shifts, motions, and weird-looking plays to get our guys ready for the point in the year they would have to stop it. We would do a lot of what we called good-on-good in training camp where we would go red-zone defense versus red-zone offense and run four plays from each spot. Those were always very competitive and fun. I think you can build team spirit in that respect.

Arians was such a gifted coach, and going against his offense helped our defense and vice versa. Over the last 12 games of the season, the offense averaged 23 points a game—plenty for a defense that was giving up 13 a game—and it seemed to find its way in Jacksonville on a humid Sunday night. We were 3–1 going into the game, and the Jacksonville Jaguars were 2–2, but they had beaten us four times in a row, most recently in the divisional round of the AFC playoffs the previous year. I did not think the Jaguars would be able to run on us the way they had in that disappointing overtime loss, even though they returned almost everyone on offense. To say we shut down the run is an understatement. Jacksonville managed just 38 rushing yards on 19 carries and only 210 yards of total offense.

Yet it did not take long for the game to take on a here-we-go-again feel. Our offense moved the ball well on the opening possession of the game when Jaguars cornerback Rashean Mathis struck again. He stepped in front of an out route and returned the interception 72 yards for a touchdown. Mathis always seemed to play his best against us. We should have drafted him just to keep him from playing against us.

Roethlisberger bounced back from the pick-six and led us right down the field for the tying touchdown. Eleven minutes into the game, Jacksonville had yet to run a play, but the score was tied. It was a funny game that way. We had 28 first downs and moved the ball all game. They had 14 first downs and were three of 13 on third down. We had two fourth-down stops. We ran 70 plays to their 54. What looked like a lopsided game on paper was 21–20 in favor of Jacksonville in the fourth quarter. Two big plays by Chris Hoke and a sack by LaMarr Woodley forced a punt that gave us the ball on our 20-yard line with six-and-a-half minutes to play. Roethlisberger started throwing and moving the ball. We passed midfield, but a silly unsportsmanlike conduct penalty after we converted on third down moved us back 15 yards.

Mewelde Moore broke loose for 27-yard run on a draw play, and Roethlisberger and Ward were clutch from there. On third and 8 from the Jaguars' 31-yard line, they connected for an 18-yard pass play. Jacksonville blitzed, and people were hanging all over Roethlisberger, but he made a great throw. Jacksonville made the mistake of coming after Roethlisberger again on third down from the 8-yard line. Against a max blitz, he threw a fade pass to Ward in the corner of the end zone.

That was huge because, even though we did not convert the two-point conversion, we led 26–21, meaning Jacksonville would need a touchdown to beat us. Not that the game was over. There were still almost two minutes to play, and the Jaguars had two timeouts. Also, Jeff Reed had gotten hurt earlier in the game so our punter, Mitch Berger, had to kick off. He squibbed the kick, and we covered it well, but the Jaguars refused to go away.

On fourth and 9 from Jacksonville's 35-yard line, quarterback David Garrard completed a 10-yard pass to keep the drive alive. The Jaguars didn't get much farther thanks to James Harrison. He beat his man for a sack on second down, and Bryant McFadden batted down a third-down pass. Jacksonville's last play never had a chance.

Our defensive line always did a great job of batting down passes—our defensive line coach John Mitchell really gave us an edge in that department—and Aaron Smith came through on fourth and 14, effectively ending the game. We were 4–1 with two nice wins following the road loss to the Philadelphia Eagles. Next up was a game against a team we knew well and an organization that I knew really well.

Big Ben

As defensive coordinator for the Pittsburgh Steelers, Dick LeBeau dealt mainly with players on his side of the ball. But he had a strong relationship with several offensive players, including quarterback Ben Roethlisberger. That goes back to when Pittsburgh selected Roethlisberger in the first round of the 2004 NFL Draft. "I've heard that Coach LeBeau was a proponent for me," Roethlisberger said.

Indeed, he was, but that is not the only reason why Roethlisberger formed such a strong bond with his fellow Ohioan. "He coached players and talked to them like men. I think so many times coaches talk down or yell at you, and it's not that he didn't raise his voice or holler, but when he spoke, you listened," Roethlisberger said. "There was respect when he spoke, and that's what I mean when I say: if I had played defense, I would have played for him in a heartbeat."

The respect between Roethlisberger and LeBeau resulted in a unique ritual when the team gathered for a prayer before games. "We would hold hands, and that was our spot," Roethlisberger said. "It meant the world to me and him. We'd always look for each other...We always held hands. I missed him when he was gone. It wasn't the same. Everybody had a special spot for Coach LeBeau, but he and I definitely had a special relationship."

—G.V.B.

6

Coaching for and against the Bengals

I ALWAYS THOUGHT I WOULD COACH AFTER MY PLAYING CAREER ENDED. I thought I knew some things that could shortcut the learning process for some pretty doggone good athletes. That's the reason I didn't want to retire after 14 years of playing and on-the-job training. I had all that wealth of information. What would I do with it if I didn't coach?

I was going to be a high school coach. Let's face it: who comes out of high school or whatever course of study they're going to follow in college and says, "Oh, I think, I'll end up in the NFL coaching?" For a kid like me from a 7,500-population town like London, Ohio, that ain't my first thought. I just figured I'd be a high school coach. I was influenced by my high school coaches and my older brother, Bob. I thought that was a pretty good way to make a living.

It would have been an honor to try to make the impact that my high school coach, Jim Bowlus, had on me and countless others. Every kid in London he ever coached would speak as highly as I do about him. He was just a very special man. He helped people understand what living the right way was. I saw his impact on some kids, who probably needed some guidance, and I just thought, *That's not a bad thing. You're getting kids at an age where they're young enough that you can still influence them.* That made the occupation really appealing to me—the teaching part of it and the interacting with kids.

Bowlus was the first of many who shaped me as a coach. I played for the great Woody Hayes at Ohio State, and he was part of that philosophical group of that era. I was drafted by the Cleveland Browns in 1959 and was on the practice field with Paul Brown. I think he's got a fairly decent coaching legacy. I later worked for him as a coach when he owned the Cincinnati Bengals.

During my 14-year NFL playing career, I was in Pro Bowls with Don Shula, Vince Lombardi, George Allen, and Tom Landry. Shula coached with the Detroit Lions at the start of my playing career—both as a defensive backs coach and a defensive coordinator. The latter was his last job before becoming head coach of the Baltimore Colts in 1963.

I got to see the best. Like when I played, I watched every player, and if he did something I liked, I tried it. If it didn't work for me, I threw it away, but if it did work, it made me better. I did the same thing in getting ready to coach. I watched all these guys and I figured there was some reason they were all winning a bunch of games. I was blessed from that standpoint of being exposed to those kinds of people. When I was 35 years old, I knew I wasn't going to play football much longer. I had a large network and started calling guys I knew who were in coaching positions and applying over the phone for a position—anywhere—to get started.

Mike McCormack, a great All-Pro tackle who had been my training camp teammate with the Browns in 1959, got hired by the Philadelphia Eagles in January 1973—shortly after I retired as a player. It was his first head coaching job. He had been an assistant coach in Washington when the Redskins won the championship.

I always wanted to coach the defensive backs if I got the chance. McCormack and I talked for awhile about my coaching future, and he said, "Well, I've got a spot for you, but it might not be what you're looking for. I want you to coach special teams." I had already told him in the first interview that I wanted to coach the defensive backs.

I said, "Okay, good enough. It's a job."

He said, "I can give you $18,000 a year."

I said, "I don't care what the salary is. I'm ready to start coaching. I'll take it."

He said, "I'll tell you what: I'll give you $20,000."

So he must have felt like he was going to have to negotiate a little bit or something. Twenty was what he had me budgeted for the whole time.

That was 1972, a long time ago. My dad was an auditor for the state and he had a good job, and I think he was working for $12,000 a year.

I made a career in coaching, and it took me far beyond Philadelphia. I had stops in Green Bay, Cincinnati, Pittsburgh, Buffalo, and Tennessee. By the time I returned to the Pittsburgh Steelers in 2004 for a second stint, I had certain tenets that guided me—particularly as a defensive coordinator. When I looked at an assignment for a particular player, I didn't care if he was a tackle, linebacker, or safety. If I didn't think I could have done a certain thing when I played, I was never going to put it in the defense. It went in the garbage can. I wasn't afraid to say I was wrong. At the same time, if you don't try new stuff, pretty soon everybody knows what you're doing.

I could never watch 11 positions, but I could have a pretty good feel of what everybody did. I always stood behind the offensive huddle in practice so I could see the defensive players' eyes and I could see them huddle, watch them break, and watch most of the defense. It was important to me to be able to look into the players' eyes. That's why I never went up into the press box for games. I never wanted to go through a phone and have someone else telling them something. The biggest thing I was looking for was: what's the look on their face? They're going to tell you more with the look in their eyes than they're going to tell you with the words that they speak.

As a coordinator you're coaching all of them, but I let the assistant coaches do their job. I wanted them to feel like they could critique or voice an opinion on anything when we were all together in the room, talking about different things defensively. But once we finished that discussion and walked out of the same room, everyone taught it the same way. You may not agree with it. But we were all going to do it together because you can't ask a bunch of athletes to be a team and a bunch of brothers unless their coaches are brothers, too.

Each assistant got to talk to the whole group. In my mind that was getting them ready to be a coordinator and a head coach. I felt like I had to know everybody's position. Before I started putting together the installation of training camp, I'd go through every technique at every position with the assistant coaches. If you keep the same staff after you've been together, you didn't have to spend as much time to make sure everybody knew what they were doing. But when you get a new coach, you have to get everyone on the same page, so that everybody is teaching the same thing and speaking the same language.

All my experience as a coach taught me many things, including how hard it is to win a game in the National Football League. Our fifth game of the season provided proof of that. The funny thing is we left Cincinnati with a 38–10 win against the Bengals. It was our seventh straight win in the city where I had coached for almost two decades, including two years as the head coach. What looked on the surface like a one-sided contest was anything but that. The contest still hung in the balance heading into the fourth quarter, even though we jumped to an early 10–0 lead and held the Bengals without a first down on their first five possessions.

We really bottled up the Bengals, who had two pretty damn good wide receivers in Chad Johnson and T.J. Houshmandzadeh. Ryan Fitzpatrick, Cincinnati's young quarterback from Harvard, had a good, quick release. When I had coached in Cincinnati, I had been around two exceptional quarterbacks in Ken Anderson and Boomer Esiason. Anderson was one of the most accurate quarterbacks who ever played. I later had the pleasure of coaching with him in Pittsburgh when he joined the Steelers' staff in 2007 as the quarterbacks coach. Boomer was a forerunner of the quarterbacks that they've got today. When Boomer would go off script and start scrambling around, something good always seemed to happen for us. He was amazing, very productive.

Fitzpatrick did not have Boomer's scrambling ability, but he did a pretty good Anderson imitation late in the second quarter. He took Cincinnati down the field with perfect reads and pinpoint passing. He started making quick, accurate throws, and we were a day late and a dollar short in terms of getting them in a get-off-the-field situation. It looked like someone else got in the quarterback's uniform because he was playing great, throwing the ball into zones and beating man-to-man with good reads. I was just trying to force them to take a field goal after they got the ball into our territory, but we were not particularly sharp. The Bengals drove 92 yards, and Fitzpatrick capped a five-minute march with a five-yard touchdown pass with 30 seconds left in the half.

That gave me some good ammunition for a little halftime talk. I didn't think the guys intentionally had a letdown after the Bengals were unable to manage any first downs on five possessions, but it was almost a subconscious thing sometimes. In those instances, which didn't happen too often, I was never shy about pointing out to them that we were pretty bad, allowing a team to start from its own 8-yard line with five minutes to go in the half and end up in our end zone.

Halftime is only 10 minutes, so you weren't going to get too philosophical. You wanted them to be aware that the same guys who held the Bengals to no first downs in five possessions were not the same guys who just gave up 92 yards. The better chance to teach and stress was Monday when you went over the game film.

I spent a lot of that time doing the teaching and showing them why something was successful and why it wasn't. I didn't spend much time hollering at them, but I would raise my voice if I thought that they weren't paying attention to me. With these guys you didn't have to do much hollering. They were their own worst critics, which is what you want as a coach. The more sincere they were about them feeling bad, the better chance of it not happening again, which is all you're looking for as a coach. That's the kind of coach I was. I was always looking to learn from whatever we didn't do well and to not let it happen again.

We were kicking off to start the second half, and it was as good a time as any to demonstrate that there wasn't going to be any more of that 92-yard drive crap. It was an important drive, and I stressed that to them. Cincinnati moved the ball a little bit and got it to third and 2 when James Harrison made a really great second-effort sack. He beat the left tackle, but the tackle kind of got a last-minute shove that kind of got Harrison off balance. Showing his athleticism Harrison kept his balance enough to get one arm on the quarterback and just yanked him down. That got us off the field on that opening drive of the second half.

On first down when we got the ball back, Mewelde Moore ran for 24 yards. We went to the no-huddle offense, which I thought was the best thing Ben Roethlisberger did, and started moving the ball. Moore had runs of 24 and 14 yards, and Roethlisberger had some good third-down passes in there. Moore scored on a 13-yard run, and I could not have been more pleased about our response after the letdown at the end of the first half. Harrison came up with a big play to get the defense off the field, and Roethlisberger and Moore led a drive that allowed us to re-establish control of the game.

After the ensuing kickoff, Fitzpatrick started to get into a rhythm. He hit a couple of play-action passes and completed a really nice pass for 20 yards on an in-cut route. The Bengals got in the red zone, but the defense immediately clamped down, forcing them to settle for a field goal that cut our lead to 17–10. Cincinnati had a chance to tie the game after it got the ball back. Fitzpatrick threw a deep ball to Johnson, and Johnson just barely missed getting to it. It just slid off his fingertips. Sometimes it just goes your way because it was literally a play of a half inch one way or the other. Lawrence Timmons and James Farrior later got us off the field when they teamed up on a real good stunt rush. They both got to Fitzpatrick at the same time and sacked him. This was as big a play as Harrison's sack at the start of the half. Cincinnati had to punt and never seriously threatened again.

Playing near where he had starred in college, Roethlisberger made sure of that. On third and 8, Roethlisberger hit Santonio Holmes with a 21-yard pass. It was really a big-time throw—one of those sideline comeback routes—that only Roethlisberger could make. There is no way you can stop it when he throws it that hard and that accurate. Roethlisberger then went play-action on a deep pass to Nate Washington for 50 yards and a touchdown. That three-play sequence—getting a sack, Roethlisberger getting a first down, and throwing a 50-yard touchdown pass—turned a close game into a 24–10 lead. That is how quickly it can change.

I got really aggressive at this stage because I didn't figure the Bengals could do much running. When they did move the ball, Fitzpatrick had been effective with quick, accurate passes. We started blitzing quite a bit, and they did not have an answer for it. On third and 12, Timmons sacked Fitzpatrick, and a poor punt gave us the ball at midfield. A pass interference call on a deep pass to Hines Ward gave us the ball at the 14-yard line, and Moore capped the short drive with a two-yard touchdown run.

Just like that it was 31–10, and we added another touchdown in the final five minutes for a 38–10 win. The game had obviously been closer than the final score indicated, but take away the drive we allowed at the end of the first half, and we played really well defensively. We sacked Fitzpatrick seven times and held the Bengals to 210 yards of total offense. Moore continued to show why he had been an excellent signing in free agency. With Willie Parker still out, he rushed for 120 yards on 24 carries and scored three touchdowns. Roethlisberger threw three touchdown passes and continued his mastery of the NFL's Ohio teams. We were 5–1 and had gone 3–0 in the AFC North.

The Bengals game showed how quickly things can change in the NFL—whether it's in game or during the season. Indeed we were riding a three-game winning streak and were on our way. Until we weren't.

Farrior's Fraternal Order

James Farrior racked up 145 tackles, forced three fumbles, and intercepted two passes for the New York Jets in 2001. It appeared to be perfect timing for a career year with free agency beckoning. But Farrior, the second linebacker taken in the 1997 NFL Draft and eighth overall, did not exactly have to fend off suitors after the Jets opted not to re-sign him. He visited the Buffalo Bills and Cleveland Browns, but each team had reservations about Farrior. "Buffalo didn't know if I could play middle linebacker because I played outside with the Jets. They ended up signing London Fletcher," he said. "Cleveland: same thing. They didn't know if I could play middle linebacker and wanted somebody bigger who had experience at that position."

The Browns homed in on Earl Holmes, who was also a free agent after back-to-back 100-plus tackle seasons with the Pittsburgh Steelers. As Farrior found out during a Pittsburgh visit, the Steelers weren't ready to let Holmes walk. "Coach Cowher told me, 'We like you. We think you'd be a good fit here, but we don't know what Earl wants to do, so we're kind of waiting on Earl. If he doesn't sign back, we would like to have you. Just give me a call before you make a decision on any team,'" Farrior recalled.

Holmes signed with the Browns, and Farrior signed with the Steelers.

A move that slipped under the radar could not have worked out better for Farrior. Or the Steelers. He flourished as an inside linebacker in the Steelers' 3-4 defense and in 2004 finished second only to Baltimore Ravens safety Ed Reed for the NFL Defensive Player of the Year award. By 2008 Farrior had established himself as the unquestioned leader of the defense and not just because of his play. He set the defense after getting play calls from Dick LeBeau and he proved to be the perfect extension of the Steelers' defensive coordinator on the field because of they were so similar in temperament. "The only weakness Dick LeBeau had was he would be too cool sometimes," said Larry Foote, Farrior's running mate at inside linebacker. "He'd take his sweet time with the calls, and you had 10 other guys yelling, 'What's the call? What's the call?' That's why Farrior was so good. He was just as cool as LeBeau. Not as cool but somewhat."

Farrior took his captain duties so seriously that they extended off the field. He opened his home every Thursday night to any teammate who wanted to get a massage or acupuncture. Sometimes he had caterers bring in dinner. The players always hung out, playing cards or doing something else together. "I thought it was something that would keep us close and keep us out of trouble," Farrior said.

His teammates said it was much more than that. "Think about that obligation, and it was something that he loved to do," cornerback Bryant McFadden said. "James just did things the right way. We all respected him not just as a football player, but also his kind heart."

It is impossible to quantify how such gatherings translated to the Steelers' on-field success. But as outside linebacker James Harrison said, "I would spend more time with those guys than my family because you had work, and then we were hanging together in the evening. You built a bond. You built an unspoken communication, which you could see out on the field."

Cornerback Deshea Townsend felt that camaraderie, too. "That's what separated us," he said. "That's the thing of everybody knowing each other's kids and genuinely caring about your brother more than you care about yourself. I know I used to say all the time: 'When one person made a play, we all made a play.' When I know you personally and when I know what you are really fighting for on a personal level, it made it really easy to go on the field with you. That really helped us out as a defense."

The closeness of the defensive players did not escape the coaches. Veteran defensive line coach John Mitchell said it showed even during practices. "You had guys that genuinely cared for each other, and the thing that I liked is they competed against each other in practice every day," Mitchell said. "They went out every day and wanted to be the best that they could be. If we were in a drill and the offense was moving the ball on us, these guys copped an attitude and said, 'We're better than this. We've got to get our act together.' Every day to them was like a game. That's what you've got to have for a great defense."

—S.B.

7

Big Blue Battle

We had the toughest schedule in the National Football League in 2008. Of our 16 regular-season games, eight came against teams that were in the playoffs the previous year and teams that had won four of the last five Super Bowls. That did not include our two games against the Baltimore Ravens, and those were some of the roughest football games we played every year.

James Farrior can tell a great anecdote about our schedule. It happened in training camp when he was talking with Dan Rooney. The organization was in the midst of monumental change after the Rooney family had been mandated by the NFL to change the ownership structure that had been in place since the team's founding by Art Rooney Sr. in 1935. "They gave us the toughest schedule out of everybody so it looks like we just have to go out and win the Super Bowl," Mr. Rooney told Farrior.

Those proved to be prescient words from an all-time great NFL owner and man. We were still a long way from making that a reality, but six games into the season, I could confidently say we had a championship-caliber defense. There are two factors you've got to have on defense if you're going to be any good. You've got to be aggressive and you've got to be able to catch up to the football because there are some fast guys you're chasing. I knew that we could run, but applicable speed is what I would call it for defenses. It doesn't do a damn bit of good if you can run fast but aren't running to the right spot or hole. Or if the guys in front of you aren't taking the proper leverage. It's got to all go together.

I would say quick speed is probably more important than straight-ahead speed in any athletic competition except the 100-meter dash. That's why Troy Polamalu was so outstanding. He had the speed, but he could apply it immediately. And all these guys not only learned where they were supposed to get to, but they also learned what they were supposed to look for. They'd be waiting there for the offensive player, and that's why they were so good.

It was a team thing, and each guy took a lot of pride in getting his part of it done. One of the things that we stressed was that it's good to run around and make some plays, but the first thing is to make sure that your specific part of the defense is taken care of. Don't worry about the other guy; he's going to get there. Take care of your job and, once you know you've got your job done, go help someone else. But don't go flying around and opening up more space than you're closing down because that just leads to big plays, which leads to points and defeats.

These guys bought into that. They were very systematic and very, very disciplined. They took it very, very much to heart if someone had a good play on us. If we lost a game, they took it hard. I could usually get the guys to trust in one another and trust in what they were doing. I believed they could do it and I think they believed I could put them in a position to get it done.

The fun part of working with these guys was just seeing how many different things they could do collectively and individually. We spent a tremendous amount of time on film study on opponents, on ourselves, and how our individual techniques were improving or sometimes sliding. If a guy sees himself doing the right thing enough times and sees the results of it during successful film study, pretty soon he becomes a pretty confident player.

This group had an unusual gift of being able to respond to the study and to apply the proper defensive moves and formations that would make it harder on opponents. Polamalu was probably as gifted at that as anybody I have ever seen. Another player right there with him was Ryan Clark. Those two safeties and the two linebackers in the middle of the field, Farrior and Larry Foote, were like having coaches on the field. They had the ability to take the stuff they were studying through the week and put it to use on Sunday.

We were our own worst critics and we set standards that we expected to make. Once I got to know players, I was always on the lookout for mental mistakes. With this group of guys, I always looked at myself first to see if I was putting too many variables into the defense. Take, for example, Clark. If he didn't have a defense down within a half an hour of installation in practice, didn't know for sure what the best way to do it was, then I was asking something that was too complex. Everybody is going to get physically defeated sometimes because you're playing against the best football players in the world. But if they were having trouble sorting the Xs and Os, then I looked at myself. I knew that they were capable of learning and executing anything. If they didn't get it, it was my fault. It was too far off the diving board, and I threw it out.

I rarely had to do that with this group. We were going to show you one thing, but most of the time we weren't going to be there when the ball was snapped. The guys liked it because we were going to attack differently from what we were showing you. They did not have carte blanche to move around. That even applied to Polamalu, though he had a lot of freedom. You can't have a defense with 11 guys, where one guy can just go wherever he wants to go. But within a certain parameter of limitations, he had a choice of more than one slot to take. Polamalu's productivity shows you that he was almost always right. If I ever thought he was getting a little too far away from home, I would just say, "Hey, how about just playing it straight?" But he was easy to coach.

As the free safety, Clark had more freedom to adjust and protect, and, of course, we called that into the defense sometimes, too. But he and Polamalu played so well off each other that their positions became interchangeable. Everything in our defense worked off stopping the run. We wanted to make offenses one-dimensional so we could get them in obvious passing situations and release our pass rushers. Through the first six games, we gave up 69.7 rushing yards per game. Only Baltimore had managed more than 100 rushing yards against us, and it needed 33 rushes to accumulate 103 yards, a 3.1 average per carry.

We were facing a pretty big challenge in our seventh game of the season and not just because the New York Giants were leading the NFL in rushing. The previous season they had pulled off one of the greatest upsets in Super Bowl history, beating the New England Patriots 17–14. Eli Manning had led an improbable touchdown drive late in the game to ruin the Patriots' perfect season. The Mannings are the only brothers to win Super Bowls as quarterbacks and they did it in back-to-back seasons. The Giants had picked up where they left off. They were 5–1 like us. Paced by their running attack, they were second in the NFL in total offense.

Before we started putting in the game plan for a marquee matchup between two of the NFL's storied franchises, we received an unfortunate reminder that there are much bigger things than football. Aaron Smith's young son, Elijah, was diagnosed with leukemia on Monday. I can't imagine anything worse than having young people in your family with serious disease. Aaron is a very devout and family-oriented man, and we all went through it with him. It was not a constant topic of conversation, but everyone knew it was a tough road, and if we could help, we would. It's like a building full of brothers, and everybody shares each other's problems and tries to be uplifting and provide a place of refuge if they need it. It's always easier to go through hardships with people you know who are on your side. People say a team is a family, and I've always believed that. That team was particularly close and rallied around Aaron.

Aaron spent the week at Children's Hospital in Pittsburgh, and Mike Tomlin left it up to him whether he wanted to play against the Giants. Tomlin reiterated that the day before the game. I told Aaron, "I'm not telling you what to do. There is no right or wrong. I know your teammates are all behind you whatever you decide."

He said, "Coach, I don't think I can really play this game. I haven't practiced all week. I haven't seen the game plan. I don't know anything about them."

I told him, "Aaron, you don't need to practice or see the game plan to go play the game. But I'm not telling you what to do. It's up to you."

We didn't know what he was going to do until Sunday morning when Aaron showed up at Heinz Field. Not only did he play, but he also played well, factoring in on a goal-line stand early in the game. It just showed how special he was as a player and as a man.

We played the game short-handed on offense. Santonio Holmes did not dress for the game after breaking a team rule, and injuries left us thin at running back. Mewelde Moore started in place of Willie Parker and again played well. He had played in Minnesota when Tomlin was the Vikings' defensive coordinator. Tomlin respected him, and he really helped us, especially this game. He scored on a 32-yard touchdown run after we held the Giants to three-and-out on the first possession of the game. We scored in four plays, so people weren't in their seats yet, and it was 7–0.

The Giants had a decided advantage in field position the rest of the way, usually starting possessions in our territory. For the game their average starting field position was the 40-yard line; ours was the 20. Our defense held up despite this disadvantage, limiting the Giants to a trio of second-quarter field goals. New York led 9–7 at halftime, and I'm sure it felt like it should have had a bigger cushion. Our red-zone defense was tremendous all game. The Giants had six opportunities in the red zone, and we kept them out of the end zone five times. Of those six they had the ball inside the 5-yard line on three of them and four times they were inside the 10.

The third quarter started as the first quarter had with us scoring a quick touchdown—this time on a 65-yard pass from Ben Roethlisberger to Nate Washington. The way our defense was playing, a 14–9 lead would have stood up in a lot of games.

But in the third quarter, we lost Greg Warren, our reliable long snapper, to a season-ending knee injury. Every team has guys that practice every week as an emergency snapper. We had a couple of guys who did it. James Harrison was one; Farrior was another. In 59 years in the league, I've only seen an instance where the emergency snapper had to go in two or three times. After another Giants field goal cut the lead to 14–12 midway through the fourth quarter, we went three-and-out and had to punt from our own end zone. That did not do Harrison any favors. Like everything Harrison did, he went all out, and when he snapped it, it soared off into space, and the Giants got a safety out of it. Nobody ever blamed Harrison. That's a skill that's not an automatic thing, and he certainly didn't get a chance to practice it much.

With the score tied at 14, we had to kick off from our own 20-yard line, and the Giants ran it back to midfield. We got them to third down and we got some pressure, but Manning threw a good pass, and they worked it down the field. The Giants finally broke through, scoring a touchdown with three minutes left in the game. Roethlisberger was not able to conjure up any of his patented late-game magic, and the Giants intercepted a last-gasp pass to preserve their 21–14 win.

I was disappointed, even though we had dealt with a lot of adversity, including losing Clark, who had played a terrific game, in the fourth quarter to an injury. My general thinking coming off the field was it had been an up-and-down start to the season. We had lost our third game to the Philadelphia Eagles and then won three more and then lost in our seventh game. We were playing pretty good football but not quite at the level that you need to win a championship.

All our stats from the game were acceptable—except that we gave up the lead in the fourth quarter. I always said to the guys: "You can't lose a lead in the fourth quarter." It just gave me an opportunity to deliver that sermon one more time. It was part of the growth process with this team. We had four turnovers and no takeaways, and in a close game, that usually tells the story.

Nobody takes a loss well, but nobody on our team carped about offense or defense. They were a very close bunch. There were games where we had to play better, and there were games when the offense had to come from behind in the fourth quarter and win it. That's team football, and you preach that. It's the Pittsburgh Steelers. It's not the offense and it's not the defense or special teams. It's what the group does.

There was never any finger pointing. In fact, there were more guys consoling Harrison because he took the loss harder than anybody. That was just the way he was wired. Even though he had been put in a tough spot at a position I'm not sure he had ever played in a game, he expected to succeed. Whatever part his errant snap played in the loss in Harrison's mind, he would more than make up for it the rest of the way.

Teammates and Tragedy

Aaron Smith mentored Brett Keisel after the Pittsburgh Steelers drafted the latter in 2002, and the defensive ends became the closest of friends and linchpins on the 2008 defense. They never wanted to meet the way they did on October 20, 2008.

Smith was at Children's Hospital of Pittsburgh after his two-year-old son Elijah got diagnosed with leukemia. Still in shock after hearing that news from longtime Steelers trainer John Norwig, Keisel got a call from his wife. Their infant son, Jacob, had just been rushed to Children's Hospital because of a bad kidney infection. When Keisel got there, he saw Smith, and they embraced. "I remember thinking, *What are the chances that your two defensive ends are in the hospital at the same time with their kids?* It was a crazy year," Smith said.

An exhausting one, too.

Smith rarely left the hospital that week, even folding his 6'5" frame into a couch at night to stay with his son. Steelers coach Mike Tomlin visited him at the hospital and told him to take as much time as he needed. He and defensive coordinator Dick LeBeau left the decision of playing that Sunday against the visiting New York Giants up to Smith. He didn't know what he was going to do even after his wife, Jaimie, persuaded him to spend Saturday night at the team hotel—if only to get away and get some sleep.

Smith played the next day while still in a state that he described as trying to find his way out of a tunnel. He recorded four tackles, and the defense played well despite Pittsburgh losing 21–14. It made several inspiring stands—none more so than when it stuffed 260-pound running back Brandon Jacobs three straight times from the Steelers' 1-yard line. "I remember thinking that's the way this is with my son," Smith said, "If there's a blade of grass, we're going to fight this thing to the end."

That defensive stand symbolized how much his teammates rallied around and played for Smith the rest of the season. "The whole team really looked up to Aaron as being our kind of leader and alpha dog," Keisel said. "You knew when you went out and played that you were playing for something a little bit more. Any time you can have those motivational factors in a sport like football, it can really move mountains."

Smith did not miss a game in 2008, and preparing for and playing in them provided an escape as Elijah went through treatment. "Sometimes that was my best therapy," he said, "just going there for the day and being around those guys, and for those hours, I didn't have to think about anything else."

Smith cherished being around LeBeau as much as anyone during that time. "We would talk on a regular basis. He would always throw those little snippets of wisdom in there," he said. "It was just like a two-liner, and you walk away and you're like, *Man, that makes so much sense* or *That really hits home*. I was having a rough day one time, and people were complaining and just coming to me. And I said, 'Coach, I don't understand why everyone wants to tell me about their problems.' He looks at me and goes, 'Sometimes people just want to unload their luggage on somebody else and have them carry it for them.' He was always there, just what I needed."

This story has a happy ending. Jacob's infection turned out not to be too serious, and Elijah beat cancer and eventually grew bigger than his father. Smith dropped weight after retiring from the NFL in 2012, Elijah added it, developing into a standout two-way lineman for North Allegheny High School, right outside of Pittsburgh. He continued his career at Indiana University of Pennsylvania (IUP). As a freshman in 2022, he was listed at 6'5", 270 pounds. "It's funny," Elijah's proud father said, "because he came home for Christmas his first year, and we were in the kitchen, and I'm like, *Man, I never thought I would be a smaller man in my own kitchen.* He's bigger than me in every aspect. God has been good to us. We have been blessed."

—S.B.

8
Election Day in D.C.

The Pittsburgh Steelers had not played in our nation's capital in 20 years, and our return to the Washington, D.C., area provided a pretty big stage. We were playing Washington, another of the NFL's storied franchises, on *Monday Night Football.* The next day was Election Day, and history would be made when Barack Obama won the presidency, becoming the first Black person to hold the highest office in the land. He would later appoint Steelers owner Dan Rooney as ambassador to Ireland.

The setting provided another reminder of how far I was from London, Ohio, a town of about 7,500 residents where I was born and came of age. Set against a bucolic backdrop, London was like a lot of Ohio towns from that time, ones whose underpinnings were faith, family, and football. All three shaped me as did the small-town values that still prevail in London.

My home was about 25 miles from Ohio State. I dreamed of Ohio State from the time I could go over to the post office lawn and play football with my older brother and his friends. They had "Keep Off The Grass" signs, so we'd take the signs and lay them off the side and put them back when we got done. The area was maybe 30 yards long by 10 yards wide. But that was the biggest field we had in the neighborhood.

I was born on September 9, 1937, so some of my earliest memories were from World War II when people not fighting overseas did their part at home through rationing. There were little tokens that they gave you, and we only got so much milk and loaves of bread and had to make it last through the week. The daily menu was planned around how much we could get from the rationing coupons.

Kids in the summer were outdoors every day, and after a week, there would be holes in the soles of our shoes because they weren't made from leather. All the leather was going to the troops overseas. We had air raid drills. Sirens would go off, and we had to douse all the lights and pull down the blinds, and air-raid monitors would come around and check everything.

The Great Depression hit in the early 1930s, and the country didn't really recover from that until World War II when there was widespread rationing. Nobody had anything when I was growing up, but I never lacked for anything because of my family. My mother, Beulah; father, Robert; and older brother, Bob, were the three huge influences in my life.

My mom was the closest thing you're ever going to see to an angel walking around on Earth. Just a compassionate, caring person with an amazing demeanor to her. Nothing fazed her. She always looked at the good things the challenges would bring our family. Mom would always find the silver lining in the cloud that was over us. She always found a way to make us laugh. Matriarch is not a strong enough word to describe her. She was the glue to the family. My mom was such a Christian woman. I just never heard her say a bad word about anybody. She was such a special person in my life.

She was so special that I would call her every night during my coaching days. She was so elated when I got nominated for the Pro Football Hall of Fame in August 2009. She was 96 years old but still very lucid. The only problem was that she conflated a nomination with induction into the Hall of Fame. I tried to explain to her that they weren't the same thing because I was afraid she'd be heartbroken if I didn't get inducted.

I saw her for the last time about a month after my nomination. The Steelers were playing in Cincinnati on September 27, and the day before, Coach Tomlin allowed me to leave early so I could go to Columbus, Ohio, for my induction into the Ohio State Varsity "O" Hall of Fame. In between receiving that honor at an awards banquet and driving to Cincinnati for team meetings on Saturday night, I stopped to see my mom. During the visit I tried to explain that I still had to go through two rounds of voting and that it was not a done deal that I would get into the Pro Football Hall of Fame. She raised a finger and said, "Charles Richard, you are going in!"

She passed away a short time later.

She proved to be right about me going into the Hall of Fame, and in August 2010, I delivered a subtle yet poignant reminder of that right before my induction speech in Canton, Ohio. As I walked to the podium, I pointed to the sky and said to myself, "Mom, you were right. We made it."

My dad taught me the will to compete and not worry about what the other guy was doing—whether he was bigger, stronger, or faster. Just keep going and play your game and you'll win your share of them.

My dad's right leg was a couple of inches shorter than his left leg. He had gotten a bad infection when he was eight years old, and it almost killed him. The infection settled in his knee, and after an operation, he had to be in a cast for more than three months. During that time his leg in the cast didn't grow, and when the cast came off, one leg was shorter than the other. He was very athletic, even though he was only 5'6".

My dad took up golf late in life and was a very short hitter. But he ended up winning our club championship in London seven times. All these guys would outdrive him by a mile, but they couldn't beat him. He just had this tremendous hand/eye coordination in his chipping and putting. As soon as I got big enough, I became his caddy. We were playing in Springfield, Ohio, and it was larger with a population of probably about 70,000 people. (London had about 7,000 then.) Dad won the Springfield City Championship one year. He was so competitive, and that provided me with my philosophical background, not worrying how big you were or how fast you were. There were other ways to get it done.

The funny thing is I grew to be 6'0" tall, which made me an outlier in my family. My mother was 5'2", and my dad had a sister who was 4'11". My grandmother, Leona LeBeau, was 5'0". One of my uncles was 6'0" tall, and somehow I got that gene. My brother, Bob, was 5'8", and while he was never the biggest guy, I always looked up to him and always tried to live up to the example he set in sports and especially in the classroom.

I've always felt so grateful to have been born into that family and what it meant. Your word was sacred. You learned truth, honesty, and consideration for other people. You got up every Sunday, went to Sunday school, and stayed for church. Then we went down to my grandmother's and had a Sunday chicken dinner. That was the biggest meal we had the whole week. It was a two-hour process because everybody would fill everybody else in on what was going on in their life that last week. I was always champing at the bit, looking at my mom and dad like, *When can I go to the golf course?*

It was a different time, and I wouldn't trade those days for anything. There weren't any televisions. We had radio and had to use our imagination there. We were always outside, and I was a big sports guy. We'd be outside shooting baskets in the winter, throwing footballs in the fall, playing baseball in the summer.

Bob was three years ahead of me, and in his senior year, his high school football team went undefeated. That was always my goal. I got to be on plenty of great teams but never an undefeated one. Our high school coach, Jim Bowlus, won 70 percent of his games in a little town with 7,500 people in central Ohio. There's not a kid who went through that school system who didn't revere Coach Bowlus. We all learned many valuable lessons from and through him.

I always thought the greatest coaching in our country takes place at the high school level because you're dealing with kids and can affect their future and life's development. If you've got some tenets you can teach, you're going to impact a lot of people's lives. Men and women who take the time to invest themselves in the youth of our nation and teach them certain principles reach more lives than any NFL coach ever could. They teach things that can't be taught in a textbook.

My senior year in high school, I got faster and bigger and had a good year, resulting in some college opportunities. West Point was one of them. A lot of people wanted me to go there, and Coach Bowlus thought that would be great. If you come out of a service academy, you're probably going to have a job for the rest of your life. I got an appointment to West Point, but Paul Dietzel, the assistant coach who had recruited me and been to London twice, left West Point that spring. He went to LSU and became a very successful head coach. After I turned down the appointment to West Point, he called me and said, "Well, since you're not going to West Point, you might as well go to the next best school in the country."

I did get an offer from LSU, but I wasn't going to go that far away from home. Not taking the West Point appointment probably turned out for the best. I don't think I would have lasted there. I had too much Jimmy Dean in me.

Ohio State had been talking to me all along, and after I ran some pretty good times in spring track my senior year, I finally ended up getting a full offer from the Buckeyes. My dad had been loving on Ohio State, and it was close enough that I could get home to Mama's cooking if I wanted. Once I received a scholarship offer, there was really no decision to make. I was going to suit up for Ohio State and the great Woody Hayes. My time in Columbus, Ohio, helped shape me, too, and was a significant stop on the journey I made from little old London to the NFL—and stages such as the one we were scheduled to play against the Washington Redskins on the first Monday in November.

We were a game ahead of the Baltimore Ravens in the AFC North, and the Redskins were only a half game behind the New York Giants in the NFC East. Washington was leading the NFL in rushing behind the dynamic Clinton Portis, who had rushed for more than 120 yards during his last five games. The only guys who had done that in the previous 50 years were Jim Brown and O.J. Simpson. That's pretty good company. Washington was really rolling under first-year head coach Jim Zorn, who had installed a West Coast offense.

We were short-handed in the secondary. Ryan Clark had played a terrific game the previous week against the Giants but got knocked out in the fourth quarter and could not play against Washington. The same was true of Bryant McFadden, who was also out with an injury. We were fortunate to get Casey Hampton and Brett Keisel back for the game, especially facing a back as hot as Portis. We dealt with different kinds of adversity in this game, starting with when fans were still probably settling into their seats at FedEx Field.

We tried an onside kick on the opening kickoff, and they got it. There was a penalty, too, giving Washington the ball on our 36-yard line. Generally speaking, if teams are going to try an onside kick, they don't tell the defensive coordinator. When Bill Cowher was the head coach, every now and then he would walk by me and say, "Just in case, Dick, be ready. We're going to onside kick this," and just kept walking. It wasn't: "Do you want to onside kick this?"

Washington ran it twice, threw an incompletion, and kicked a field goal two minutes into the game. On our first possession, Ben Roethlisberger threw a third-down pass that was tipped and intercepted. Then Washington had it on our 30-yard line, and adversity was always one of my lecturing points. It doesn't matter what the situation is when you go onto the field. Defend the last blade of grass and make them kick the field goal if it's down on our one-inch line. Our guys were fantastic in the red zone. They were fantastic on the goal line.

They forced a three-and-out, and Washington had to settle for another field goal. Our guys were pretty confident when they came off the field that second time, and a couple of minutes into the game, Washington had all of the points it was going to get in the nationally televised game.

The next time Washington got the ball, Portis broke free for a 22-yard run. That was the longest run we had given up to that point of the season. They got to our 41-yard line, but James Farrior made a rush and knocked down a pass with a real good move to force a punt. Farrior was such an underrated player. He could blitz. He could cover. He had instincts. He was very fast. He almost never missed a play. As an inside linebacker, he could really cover a lot of ground, and so could Larry Foote.

There were six straight series where the offenses went three-and-out. Washington only managed three first downs in the first half and no third-down conversions. Roethlisberger got the offense going midway through the second quarter when he hit Hines Ward with a 45-yard pass off play-action. That led to our first points: a field goal that cut Washington's lead in half.

Another key special teams player stepped up later in the quarter. After a Washington three-and-out, Andre Frazier, who was a backup linebacker, made a hell of a punt block. Frazier's block was big because we had not done much offensively outside of Roethlisberger's long pass to Ward. We got the ball on Washington's 31-yard line, and Roethlisberger hit a couple of passes, including a hook on third and 8 to Ward near the end zone.

It looked like Ward got over the goal line, but they ruled him down at about the 3-yard line. Roethlisberger ran a sneak for a touchdown right at the end of the first half. After Roethlisberger scored and the offense came off the field, he ran into the locker room. We all wondered, *What the hell*? I figured that maybe he got hit on that sneak, but it turned out his shoulder had been bothering him. He didn't come out with us after halftime.

I wasn't too worried, and not just because our defense was playing so well. We had the best quarterback situation of any team I have ever been with and the best I've ever seen in the NFL. We had Roethlisberger, of course, and we had picked up Byron Leftwich during the preseason, and he had started 44 games in the National Football League. He was a very tested quarterback. We also had Charlie Batch, who also had started a bunch of games in the NFL. You were never out of a game if any of those guys were in there. They could all play and win.

Leftwich proved as much in a homecoming for the Washington, D.C., native. He played the entire second half and finished with a sparkling passer rating of 145.8. We got the ball to start that second half, and Leftwich threw a 50-yard pass to Nate Washington to set up a one-yard touchdown run by Willie Parker. We missed the extra point but extended our lead to 16–6.

A little later in the quarter, we all but put the game away. The Redskins got something going with two first downs, the second of which crossed midfield. They ran a play-action pass the first time they got across the 50-yard line, and we were ready for it. When any team that was struggling against us even got close to the 50-yard line, I always expected a play-action pass to try to get a quick strike. That's just a tendency that offensive teams display. Chris Hoke made a real good play getting off his block and tipped the ball, and Deshea Townsend picked it off. That was the first interception that Jason Campbell had thrown that year, and it effectively ended the game.

Leftwich punctuated his big game with a five-yard touchdown pass to Santonio Holmes and the final score in our 23–6 win. Once again our depth really stood out. Leftwich played lights out, and Ty Carter played every snap at free safety in place of Clark and had a great game. He proved that he, too, could mix and match with Troy Polamalu. And I can never say too much about guys like Hoke and Travis Kirschke and Nick Eason. They gave us superior depth along the defensive line and played a lot. Those guys knew what they had to do, and our defense didn't miss a beat.

The NFC East was a pretty damn good division that year, and this was one of our better defensive games. We held Portis to 51 of Washington's

60 rushing yards and sacked Campbell seven times. James Harrison and LaMarr Woodley combined for two-and-a-half sacks, which was pretty typical production for them. The win improved our record to 6–2 at the midway point of the season, and one statistic really jumped out at me. Opposing offenses had gone three-and-out against us about a third of the time. That is mind-boggling and was a lot of fun. I could only hope matching wits with Peyton Manning in our next game would be as fun. But fun was not generally associated with playing against one of the best quarterbacks in NFL history.

Buckeye Brethren

During Dick LeBeau's playing days at Ohio State, it was a golden era for sports. Future Washington Senators star Frank Howard had earned All-American honors while playing men's basketball *and* baseball for the Buckeyes. He and LeBeau were good friends, and Howard went on to a distinguished career in professional baseball, clubbing 382 career home runs in the major leagues while earning the nickname "Capital Punisher." The Buckeyes' football team won a national championship in 1957 while LeBeau played offense and defense. The basketball team won one in 1960 with players like Jerry Lucas, John Havlicek, and a reserve forward named Bobby Knight.

"The General" became synonymous with college basketball. He won three national championships at Indiana University and 902 Division I games—among the most in NCAA history. Knight and LeBeau formed a lifelong friendship dating back to their Ohio State days. "Dick was in school as a senior when I was there as a freshman and then he came back to work on his degree after that while he was playing with the Lions," Knight said. "We had a couple of classes together and just got to know one another and really got along well. Dick was a heck of a basketball player. I think he could have played basketball at that level. I think that during the time I was at Ohio State he may have been the very best athlete that was there."

That is high praise, considering the star power across all sports in Columbus during that era, including Havlicek and Lucas.

LeBeau and Knight might not have become as close as they did had LeBeau not changed majors. LeBeau started as an accounting major but switched to physical education when he realized he wanted to go into coaching after his playing days were over. That led to the classes he had with Knight during NFL offseasons while he was finishing his degree. When LeBeau was back in Columbus, Ohio, he and Knight sometimes dropped in on LeBeau's Buckeyes coach, the legendary Woody Hayes. "Bobby wanted to go down and see Coach Hayes every day, and I said, 'Bobby, he's the head football coach at Ohio State. He's got better things to do than sit and chat with us for awhile,' But I would take him down," LeBeau said. "I've always wondered if that was a good idea taking him down there to see Coach Hayes."

While Hayes coached the football team, the golf team was led by Jack Nicklaus and Tom Weiskopf. Each went on to decorated professional career, and Nicklaus' 18 major championships are a record that will likely never be broken. LeBeau played golf with each of them. He also hooped quite a bit with the Buckeyes, especially Havlicek. "The only guy who wouldn't play was Jerry Lucas. He was too good," LeBeau said of the player who was a three-time, first-team All-American. "It was good to compete with guys who were good athletes. I played a lot of basketball with John Havlicek, and he didn't shoot it any better than I did. I wasn't going to rebound with him or anything like that, but I could play any of the shooting games with him."

LeBeau and Havlicek also bonded over their love of football. The latter had been an all-state football player in Ohio along with excelling in basketball. He did not play football at Ohio State, but that did not stop the Cleveland Browns from selecting him in the seventh round of the 1962 NFL Draft. The Boston Celtics took Havlicek with the seventh *pick* of the 1962 NBA Draft, which settled the matter.

Or did it? "He called me one day and said, 'I want to talk to you.' I drove over to Ohio State, which was only 25 miles away, and we met," LeBeau said. "He told me that he really wanted to play football. I said, 'Well, John, I don't know if that's a good idea because you're going to be a great basketball player. You're never going to be a great scorer, but you're a tremendous defensive player. You're a great floor player, a great rebounder, and the Celtics have shooters, they've got defenders, they've got break runners. You'll fit in perfect in that system and you'll play there as long as you want to play. I don't know why you would want to jeopardize that by stepping on the football field. You could have one play, and your basketball career is over.'"

Havlicek did not listen to LeBeau—on several fronts. He went to training camp with the Browns and played in several preseason games before getting released. Once he focused on basketball full time, he became a prolific scorer while making 13 All-Star Games and helping the Celtics win eight NBA Championships. Havlicek scored 26,395 career points, which is still the most in the Celtics' illustrious history. LeBeau laughs when recalling how he was right about Havlicek being a great NBA player but tossed up the prediction equivalent of a brick when telling his friend that he would not be a big-time scorer in Boston. "Looking back," LeBeau said, "I was blessed to be around some pretty special athletes."

LeBeau is known as a great defensive back, but during his playing days at Ohio State he was a two-way player, also lining up as a halfback on offense. "I scored the first two-point conversion for Ohio State University," LeBeau said. "The rule came in when I was playing there, and I think we ended up in an 8–8 tie with Wisconsin. I caught a pass believe it or not."

Actually, it's not so far-fetched. LeBeau led the Buckeyes in receiving his junior and senior season. He caught seven passes for 57 yards in 1957 and eight for 58 yards in 1958. For comparison's sake, LeBeau's 115 receiving yards in those combined seasons were less than what Buckeyes All-American wideout Marvin Harrison Jr. had in five different games in 2022. "It was a different offense," LeBeau said. "Believe me."

That had as much to do with the coach as it did the era. Hayes did not have much more use for the forward pass than he did anything having to do with the University of Michigan. Hayes once famously said: when you pass, three things can happen, and two of them are bad. Hayes' teams reflected his no-frills approach to football and tougher-than-armadillo-skin demeanor.

Hayes did not bristle at characterizations of his offenses as three yards and a cloud of dust. He embraced them as LeBeau found out while playing halfback for the Buckeyes. "When we went to spring training, he had a piece of rope cut that was 3.3 yards, and you carried that in your notebook," LeBeau said. "You had it hanging from your book in your bed. His theory was you get 3.3, 3.3, 3.3. That's 9.9, and some place you're going to get that extra tenth and you have a first down. That's how he presented his philosophy of running the ball."

The Buckeyes won a national championship in LeBeau's junior season, and he played both ways as a halfback and cornerback his senior season. "I averaged almost 57 minutes a game, so you had to be in pretty good shape," he said. "We didn't want to come out of the games."

—G.V.B.

9

Peyton's Place

My second stint as the Pittsburgh Steelers' defensive coordinator coincided with a time of superb quarterback play in the NFL. That is not unlike most eras, but it did not make my job any easier. At least I only had to go up against Ben Roethlisberger, one of the elite quarterbacks from that time, in practice. I saw more than my share of two quarterbacks who are on the short list of the best of all time: Tom Brady and Peyton Manning.

They were both fantastic players. I'd say Brady is the best ever because of the number of championships that he's got. My thought about Manning is he was a bigger part of the offense wherever he was. He kind of ran the whole damn thing. Not that Brady didn't check off or wasn't a tremendous field general, but with Manning 90 percent of the offense wasn't called until he got up to the line of scrimmage and started looking things over a little bit. I just thought he had a bigger impact on what the opponents did. If either one of them got a pre-snap read on what you were doing, you were a cooked goose. You had to practice deception on them as much as you practiced exactly what you were going to do in the game. If you were trying to take a guy like Rob Gronkowski out of it, you had to hide the way you were doing it or you'd lose every down. I've got a lot of respect for both of those quarterbacks. They got me more than I got them. That's why I cherish so much the couple of times that we got them.

One of those came in the 2005 AFC Divisional Playoffs. It was one of the wildest wins in Steelers' history. Maybe one of the greatest, too. The Indianapolis Colts had flirted with a perfect record for most of the regular season. One of their wins came against us in the RCA Dome on a Monday night, a 26–7 victory near the end of November. Few outside Pittsburgh gave us a chance to win when we again traveled to Indianapolis in the middle of January.

What many seemed to overlook was that when they beat us in the regular season we had quite a few guys hurt. Roethlisberger had missed some games and was playing hurt. When we got all of those guys back, we were a totally different team. We got rolling in that final stretch of the season and won four straight games to qualify for the playoffs. We played the Cincinnati Bengals in the wild-card round. They had won the division, and we were not a whole team when we had played them in early December. We avenged that 38–31 loss at Heinz Field, but even our 31–17 win seemed to come with a caveat since Bengals quarterback Carson Palmer had been knocked out of the game early with a knee injury.

The next week something struck me when I was on the field during pregame warm-ups in the RCA Dome. I thought—and I'll never forget this—*Well, these guys are a great team, they've got a great quarterback, but they're kind of ripe for picking here if we can just play a good football game.* You could just see that they thought they could beat anybody.

The key to beating Indianapolis was getting pressure on Manning. When putting together game plans, I didn't care so much about how many different protections opposing teams had. I tried to isolate when we had a reasonable chance of predicting which protection we were going to get when it was a crucial point of the game. What were they going to block you with? I thought they were a little weak up the middle with the protection patterns they were running. I came up with what we called a "Triple Middle." We just sent the kitchen sink up the middle. James Farrior and Larry Foote were quick and fast, and Casey Hampton was a full-time bulldozer. The movement in the middle pretty much negated whatever Manning was trying to do back there. Every time he looked up, Steelers were in his lap. It was a good idea because of the people I had running it, and those three guys particularly made it work.

The cave-in brought into play either Joey Porter or Clark Haggans on the outside. If Manning tried to bail out to the outside, it brought them into the rush. They were running around their guys pretty fast. It was something the Colts hadn't seen and it worked because of the players. We sacked Manning five times, and after the game, Pittsburgh simply referred to that blitz as "Indy."

I didn't call it early because I thought it was going to be good. As the game went on, there were a couple of situations where I thought they would probably have that protection on. You can design defenses, and they may look good, but it's the impact, the timing, the explosiveness that the individual players put into that blitz that make them effective. Our guys just hit it with so much power and just buried their blockers. The Colts had hats on hats, but they couldn't block anybody, starting with Porter. Our offense came out firing and gave us a 14–0 lead. Indianapolis trailed 21–18 near the end of the game when we sacked Manning twice in three plays, including the final one on the Colts' 1-yard line with just under two minutes to play.

It was Jerome Bettis time, but Bettis, who never fumbled, fumbled on first down. Their safety Nick Harper picked it up and almost ran it all the way back for a touchdown that would have beaten us. Somehow Roethlisberger got Harper on the ground. I will never know how. That's the greatest play I've ever seen a quarterback make in a defensive role.

The Colts had the ball at midfield, and there certainly are quarterbacks I'd rather face in that situation than Manning. He naturally went after Bryant McFadden, our rookie cornerback. We had drafted him in the second round, and as the season went along, he started playing a lot of football for us since we used five, sometimes six defensive backs. Coaches are definitely show-me people, and until you do, I'm going to keep my eye on you pretty close.

McFadden knocked down two passes—one of them in the end zone—and he made a good open-field tackle on another play. His play forced the Colts to attempt a field goal that I had absolutely no doubt they would make. They had a kicker who never missed. Strange things can happen in a football game, and Mike Vanderjagt did miss.

Of course, the rest is history as we went on to win Super Bowl XL in Detroit, hoisting the Lombardi Trophy for the first time since the Steel Curtain dynasty.

I didn't worry too much about McFadden after that game because if he had the moxie, the stamina, and the skill to hold up in that situation against that offense and that quarterback, he was going to be okay. It was just a matter of giving him time to learn everything. A couple of years later, he was just more confident, more sure of himself. He really stepped up early in 2008 when Deshea Townsend was sidelined with an injury and gave us three high-caliber starting cornerbacks with Townsend and Ike Taylor. We needed more than them during the season because of injuries. Will Gay, a second-year cornerback, developed very quickly, which was crucial. We also got solid play from Anthony Madison and Fernando Bryant, who were signed during the season. We don't get to the Super Bowl without that great cornerback depth.

After a really solid win against Washington, we returned home to play Indianapolis for the first time since that playoff win that will forever live in Steelers lore. The Colts were only 4–4, but they were still the Colts, which means they were loaded on offense. They had probably the best wide receiver duo in the NFL in Marvin Harrison and Reggie Wayne. Tight end Dallas Clark was a heck of a receiver, too, and a really tough matchup. Edgerrin James keyed their rushing attack, and as in 2005, everything started with Manning.

The Colts had a dynamic safety of their own in Bob Sanders, and their defense had been playing pretty good football; they were just having trouble on third down. Other than that, they would have had a much better record than 4–4.

We had a murderous schedule and were just getting into the meat of it. We still had the Dallas Cowboys, Baltimore Ravens, and Tennessee Titans three weeks in a row on the back end. I think the way the schedule was built gave our team championship mettle. You're not going to play a schedule like we had and win them all. It just helped toughen us up for the playoffs because most of those games were going to go down to the fourth quarter and the last couple of possessions. It was a great spot in the season for us to play a quarterback like Manning.

Roethlisberger had gotten knocked out of the Washington game and did not practice all week because of a sore shoulder that bothered him throughout the season. He sure looked good after the opening kickoff. He led a 10-play, 62-yard touchdown drive and really looked sharp on a 23-yard completion to Santonio Holmes. That set up a one-yard touchdown run by Mewelde Moore.

It was a great start, but our lead was short-lived. Manning threw a 65-yard touchdown pass to Wayne on Indianapolis' fourth play from scrimmage. It was the first big play our defense gave up that season.

It was also a fluke.

We got pressure on Manning, and Taylor had Wayne covered perfectly. Taylor ducked under Wayne to intercept the ball. Instead of catching the ball, he batted it up in the air, and it bounced off his shoulder pads and hit Wayne in stride. Ryan Clark, coming from center field, got over there and would have been in position to make a play. But with the ball getting tipped, he ended up overrunning the play, and Wayne scored.

Hines Ward showed that Harrison and Wayne weren't the only great wide receivers in this game. He caught eight passes for 112 yards. One of them was a fantastic catch that kept a drive alive early in the second quarter, one that Moore finished with another one-yard touchdown run. Jeff Reed kicked a field goal later in the quarter and he was just so consistent that season. He was particularly reliable at home, and Heinz Field is notoriously one of the most difficult places to kick in the league. He is another guy that we probably would not have won a championship without. On a lot of those have-to-have kicks, he delivered. It was 17–7, and there were only four minutes to go in the half.

On Indianapolis' next possession, Troy Polamalu made a great break on a third-down pass and he might have scored had he held onto the ball. Still, we seemed to be firmly in control after getting the ball back late in the second quarter and holding a 10-point lead. On third and 2 from our own 16-yard line, Roethlisberger threw a deep pass, and Indianapolis cornerback Keiwan Ratliff undercut the route and picked it off.

The Colts ended up with the ball on our 30-yard line with a minute and 24 left in the half. That's what the defense is there for: to answer the bell in an adverse situation, and this was a must-stop situation. I felt confident that we would limit them to a field goal. They got to our 2-yard line but had a third down with no timeouts. Manning jammed in the pass for a touchdown. That was an opportunity we had to save four points for the team. We didn't get it done, but Manning's tough down there.

They came out of halftime with a different concept on offense: shorter, quicker passes, and Manning was on. He hit his first six passes of the second half to get the Colts to our 18-yard line. Most of the plays were pretty well defended and contested. We stopped them on third down, and Adam Vinatieri kicked a field goal to tie the game. They ended the first half with a touchdown and then opened the third quarter with that field goal to tie the game at 17.

Later in the quarter, it was déjà vu all over again, as Yogi Berra might say. Taylor broke underneath a pass intended for Wayne, and it was a beautiful play. He kind of bumped into Wayne, and it kicked off Taylor's left arm, bounced up in the air, and Wayne caught the damn thing for a key first down. We would have had them punting from their own 27-yard line. It's amazing that two plays like that happened in the same game and involved the same two players. When you're hot, you're hot is the axiom there.

At the beginning of the fourth quarter, our offense made another really good drive. On third and 2, Roethlisberger hit Ward with a 17-yard pass. We picked up another first down, and two good Moore runs put us at the Indianapolis 5-yard line. On first down we picked up four yards. We ran it twice and didn't get to the line of scrimmage. We kicked the field goal to take the lead, which was the right thing to do, and went ahead 20–17. We felt like we were in pretty good shape. We were moving the ball, and they weren't.

The Colts went three-and-out and had to punt it right back to us, and we got the ball at the 30-yard line. On third and four, Roethlisberger threw a slant to Holmes, and Tim Jennings made a really good play to pick off the pass. There were only five minutes left in the game. They had great field position like they did at the end of the first half. This was another shot for us to get off the field—or at least make them kick a field goal.

They picked up a first down on our 17-yard line with three minutes left and then came our worst play of the game. We missed our angles, and our execution was poor. That didn't happen often, but it did here at the most inopportune time. We blitzed, and Manning sidestepped a little bit, and we didn't get running back Dominic Rhodes covered in the flat, and he scored. That made the score 24–20. We got the ball down to the Indianapolis 27-yard line, but we had used all of our timeouts, and Roethlisberger threw a pass that they intercepted in the end zone.

The turnover battle decided this game, as it so often did. We had three and did not force any. We only allowed 290 yards of total offense—our goal was always to hold the opposition to under 300—but came up short in our goals of takeaways and points allowed.

Looking back, I think that game had as much to do as any with us becoming world champions. We started to do a lot of things really right in crucial situations in that game. In a one-play, four-point game, whoever happens to be on the right side of that one play wins it. I think it was a great experience for our team. They say you can learn as much from a loss as from a win. I'm not sure of that, but I do think that game in the end benefitted our growth. We were starting to look like a championship team. We answered adversity, and our offense had several really good drives. When the playoffs came, we were battle tested and ready to win because of losses like this one.

When Potsie Went Down

His nickname is "Potsie," which his mother gave him as a toddler because of his protruding belly and her love of the sitcom *Happy Days*. Had his Pittsburgh Steelers career been the only consideration, James Farrior's nickname would have been "Rocky."

Farrior was a rock in the middle of the Steelers' defense from the time he signed with Pittsburgh in 2002 as a free agent until retiring following the 2011 season. During his 10-year Steelers career, Farrior started 154 of 160 regular-season games and never missed a postseason contest. His greatness started with his availability, something that turned what could have been a dicey situation into a funny (if somewhat disputed) story.

The Steelers were trying to win their first Lombardi Trophy since 1979 when disaster seemed to strike in the 2005 Super Bowl against the Seattle Seahawks. Farrior was rushing the quarterback late in the first half of a close game when he landed his on his shoulder—with an offensive tackle on top of him. "It just snapped," said Farrior, who was eventually diagnosed with a third-degree sprain. "I tried to play another play, but I couldn't move shit. I ran off to the sideline and I told [head trainer John] Norwig and Dr. [Jim] Bradley. We sprinted to the locker room, and they examined the injury from every physical angle and determined the ailment was a matter of me dealing with some discomfort. With their okay I was not going to let a little pain keep me out of the Super Bowl."

The Steelers were holding a tenuous 7–3 lead when the player, who set the defense after getting the play call from Dick LeBeau, got hurt. "I was like, 'I have to hurry and get back' because Foote and Clint Kriewaldt had a difference of opinion as to how we would fill my inside linebacker spot. Larry didn't want to leave his usual position, and Clint didn't want to set the defense. Luckily, I got back out there to end the chaotic situation between my teammates. It was so funny."

Whatever transpired on the sidelines indeed ended up as a moot point. Farrior played the rest of the way with a bum shoulder, and the Steelers beat the Seahawks 21–10, a victory that ended the franchise's Super Bowl drought.

The game—and especially the "Who's On First" incident—underscored the importance of Farrior to the Steelers' defense. "James set everything in motion with his checks and calls at the line of scrimmage," LeBeau said. "He was the hub of the wheel, so much so that both men in the normal rotation did not really want to go into the Super Bowl and shoulder the responsibility. To this day when the group gets together, there is a lot of laughter and finger pointing when reliving the moment of that game. However, at the time it was no laughing matter."

—S.B.

10
Super Bowl Dress Rehearsal

I played for the Detroit Lions from 1959 to 1972. *(Detroit Lions)*

I participate in a photo shoot when I played defensive back for the Detroit Lions. *(Detroit Lions)*

I play for Ohio State during the era of the great Woody Hayes. *(The Ohio State University)*

I participate in one of the 185 games I played for the Detroit Lions. *(Detroit Lions)*

My jumping ability was one reason I was able to record 62 career interceptions. *(Detroit Lions)*

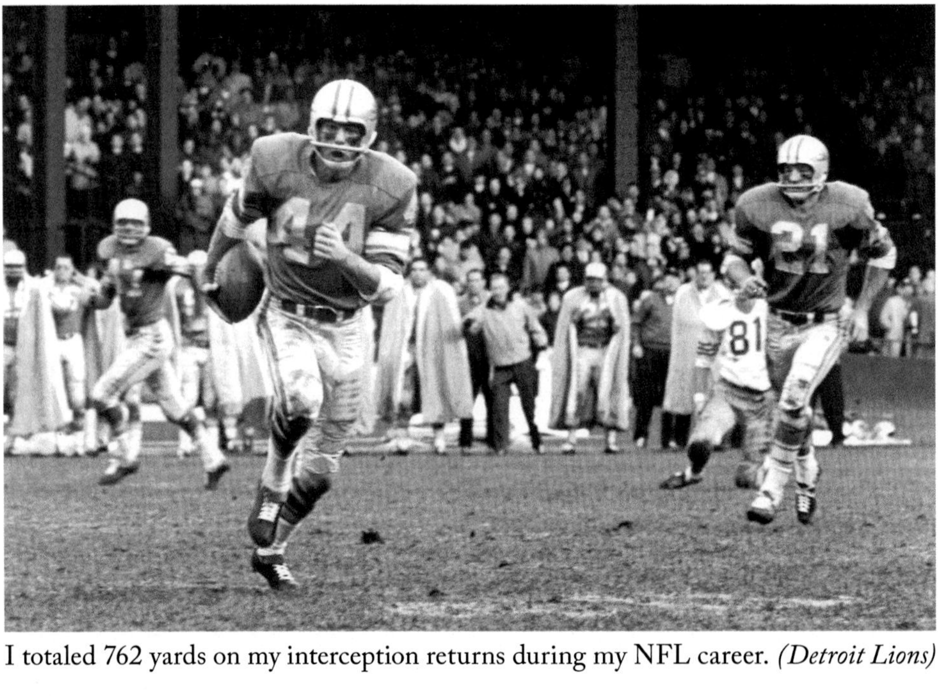

I totaled 762 yards on my interception returns during my NFL career. *(Detroit Lions)*

I battle Green Bay Packers receiver Max McGee for a reception. *(Detroit Lions)*

I battle St. Louis Cardinals receiver Sonny Randle for a pass. *(Detroit Lions)*

I display my nose for the football against the Cleveland Browns. *(Detroit Lions)*

I ripped the seat of my pants out in a game against the Dallas Cowboys, and that incident ended up getting spoofed in *MAD* magazine. *(George Von Benko)*

I pose with my Detroit Lions teammates (from left to right): Yale Lary, Gary Lowe, and Dick "Night Train" Lane. *(Detroit Lions)*

I stand next to Dick "Night Train" Lane, and three of my Detroit Lions teammates—Pat Studstill, Bruce Maher, and Gary Lowe—kneel. *(Detroit Lions)*

My late mother, Beulah, whose love shaped me in every way possible, joined me when I was honored in my hometown of London, Ohio, in 2009. *(Dick LeBeau)*

Known for his long locks, Troy Polamalu was an absolute pleasure to coach. *(Pittsburgh Steelers)*

I receive the key to the city of Pittsburgh alongside my longtime friend, Bill Priatko, who was my first pro roommate while I was with the Cleveland Browns. *(Dick LeBeau)*

Troy Polamalu makes one of his signature big plays in a rivalry game against the Baltimore Ravens. *(Pittsburgh Steelers)*

Linebacker James Harrison's interception in Super Bowl XLIII was one of the best plays in NFL history. *(Pittsburgh Steelers)*

James Harrison eludes several Arizona Cardinals, including the great Larry Fitzgerald (11), on his interception return just before halftime. *(Pittsburgh Steelers)*

One thing I love about James Harrison's signature Super Bowl touchdown is it shows our defensive teamwork, including the block by linebacker LaMarr Woodley (56). *(Pittsburgh Steelers)*

James Harrison had reason to be exhausted after his interception return. He probably ran 150 yards on the play because he was weaving and jumping over people before crashing into the end zone. Fortunately, he was probably the best-conditioned athlete on our team. *(Pittsburgh Steelers)*

I still don't know how Santonio Holmes caught the Super Bowl XLIII-winning touchdown. Several things in that game were meant to be, and my guardian angel shined down on us that night through Holmes and Ben Roethlisberger. *(Pittsburgh Steelers)*

LaMarr Woodley helps seal our victory during the final seconds of Super Bowl XLIII. *(AP Images)*

My older brother, Bob, gave me a copy of the *Buckeye Sports Alumni* magazine in April 2022 after we had played a round of golf. "Read this," he told me. "You might find it interesting."

What I found was one of the greatest sports compliments I have ever received, and it had nothing to do with football. The author of the article had asked Jack Nicklaus about playing golf with other athletes while at Ohio State and who he thought was the best golfer from another sport. He said, "I would have to say Dick LeBeau was probably the best of them."

It tickled the heck out of me. My dad, who had been a terrific amateur player and instilled in me a love for the game, would have been tickled, too. To say I was surprised after reading what Nicklaus said is an understatement. He had played with some pretty damn good golfers before he became…well…Jack Nicklaus. One of them was my friend Bob Hoag, who had been Nicklaus' partner in the Pebble Beach Pro-Am for years.

I had the privilege of playing with Nicklaus and Tom Weiskopf, who is also in the World Golf Hall of Fame, when we were at Ohio State together. When I played with either one of them, I just tried to not hold them back. I guess I did okay in that regard. I'm not sure Nicklaus' record of 18 major championships will ever be broken. Tiger Woods has 15 of them, but it's hard to see him getting to 18 with age and past injuries working against him. Nicklaus' dominance helped popularize professional golf. Arnold Palmer took that popularity to another level because he appealed to sports fans who weren't otherwise interested in golf. I got to play with him two times and I saw him four or five times at training camp, which is located in his hometown of Latrobe, Pennsylvania. He was always great to me and always very flattering to me about the role I played with the Pittsburgh Steelers. I was always very proud of that.

I had a chance to see what made Arnie…well…Arnie while I was playing for the Detroit Lions. I attended what was then called the Carling World Open at Oakland Hills Country Club, a revered course that has hosted its share of major championships and a Ryder Cup. I followed Palmer, and it was coming down to the last hole, which in those days was a 470-yard hole and puts into perspective how much golf has changed. This was before metal club heads and when players still used balata golf balls, which did not fly nearly as far as today's golf balls.

The members played the last hole as a par-5, but it was par-4 for the Carling Open, making it a really long hole even for the best players in the world. In those days even after a good drive, they still had to use a four- or five-iron to get the green. Palmer was one shot behind Al Balding, one of the first Canadian pros to come down and really be successful on the PGA Tour. Palmer hooked his tee shot a bit on No. 18, and it landed in heavy rough. He went in there with an iron and he slashed that ball, and grass flew up all around. He hit the ball flush, and the doggone ball took two bounces on the green and hit the pin. It was amazing. He needed a birdie to tie for the lead and he almost made an eagle. He made the birdie putt, and I always wondered what in the hell he hit to get that ball out of that long grass.

When I had the chance to play with him, I said, "Arnie, at Oakland Hills in 1962, your second shot hit the pin, and you had to have a 3 to get into a playoff. I've always wondered what club you hit on that shot. You made that 3, and I'll never forget that shot. Do you remember what you hit there?"

He said, "Oh yeah, I hit a 6-iron, and Balding beat me in a playoff."

I was flabbergasted that he would remember the club he hit on that shot. That was a great story. He was just magnetic. If you watched him golf, it was like watching Picasso paint. He was poetry in motion and was never out of a match. He told me, "Dick, if I could see a way, I was going to take it. I didn't always make it, but if I could see a way, I was going to take it." That was the way he played golf. He only knew one way: charge. He was the most magnetic golfer ever. He was a movie star.

After we won the Super Bowl in Detroit, Palmer's longtime right-hand man, Doc Giffin, called Steelers offensive coordinator Ken Whisenhunt and me and said that Palmer would like to play golf with us at Latrobe Country Club. They set it up, and when we got there, Palmer and his playing partner were on the putting green waiting on us. There were no practice balls, putting, or anything else. We just parked the car, got the golf clubs out, and played.

Palmer made you feel like you were just playing with a regular guy. On the 12th hole, he asked us if we wanted to have a beer with him after we finished golfing. Who says no to that? I looked at Whisenhunt. *Is he serious? Would we like to talk to Arnold Palmer after we play golf?* When we finished playing, we went over to Palmer's house, and he showed us around both of his houses. His wife, Kit, took us around the new house they had just built. It was really a great day.

It was such an unbelievable experience that I kind of had to pinch myself. I even called Whisenhunt afterward. "Was I daydreaming, or did we just get done playing with Arnold Palmer and then visit with him at his house?"

He said before laughing, "Dick, I was just reaching for the phone to call you to see if it really happened."

What does Palmer have to do with the 2008 Pittsburgh Steelers? Troy Polamalu. Like with Palmer, you could see he was doing things nobody else could do. He had a flair for it that was just fun to watch. They're from a different era and a different sport, but some guys just sway the masses with the way they perform, their particular skill. Both were guys you won't see for another hundred years. Polamalu was one of those players. The opposing coach always told the quarterback never to throw the ball until you know where he is—at least to start with. He is one of the best defensive players ever.

I think we had the best safety duo in the league when Polamalu and Ryan Clark played together. Clark reminded me a lot of Darren Perry, whom I had coached as a defensive backs coach and then defensive coordinator during my first stint with the Steelers. Perry was an excellent player, the kind of guy you knew would be a great coach. He had great feet and was tough and a real good tackler. He and Clark were like having coaches on the field. They could incorporate the whole defense just with a couple of words because they knew where everybody went every snap. They were two of the better safeties that I got to coach.

Clark's importance on the back end of our defense was magnified in 2008 given all the injuries we had at cornerback. Going into our 10th game, we were down two of our top three cornerbacks with Deshea Townsend and Bryant McFadden out with injuries. That did not necessarily bode well with the San Diego Chargers visiting. Philip Rivers entered the game with the second best passer rating in the NFL, and San Diego had one of the best running backs in the league in LaDainian Tomlinson. They had a real power offense, but we had an ally that day with the weather. With the windchill it was 26 degrees, and snow blew on and off during the late-afternoon game.

It didn't take long for Polamalu to make one of those magician plays that had become his signature. On the first possession of the game, Rivers threw a pass to the left flat where Ike Taylor was in coverage. The ball got tipped, and Polamalu dove and got his hand underneath the ball. He had the presence of mind to cup his hand enough that he could angle it back to him and secure the catch a fraction of an inch from the ground. The play was challenged by San Diego, but it was upheld.

I can recall Polamalu making three to five plays like that in his career, plays that no one could ever make unless they were just an unusual connection of speed and athleticism. It was an amazing play, and the more times they replayed it, the more times you couldn't figure out how he did it. His fourth interception of the season gave us the ball at the Chargers'

41-yard line, but we could not take advantage of the excellent field position. We moved the ball a little but missed a field goal.

The Chargers seized momentum by putting together a drive that Tomlinson capped with a six-yard touchdown run. Twenty-four of those yards came on penalties. Naturally, being a defensive coach, I thought they were very questionable calls, but that is football.

Ben Roethlisberger went no-huddle on the next drive, and I always liked it when Roethlisberger went no-huddle. He was one of the best ever at running that style of offense. It usually resulted in us moving the ball, and we did here. We had a first down inside the 5, and it got to fourth and 1, and we didn't make it. So they got the ball inside their 1-yard line. We always stressed really hard to the defense: when you've got guys backed up like that, if we do a good job, the team will end up getting points out of it. Sure enough, James Harrison made a great pass rush and sacked Rivers in the end zone and caused a fumble. It resulted in a safety because the ball went out of the end zone.

It was Harrison's 12th sack of the season. Less than two years since becoming a starter, he had become one of the best outside linebackers in the NFL and maybe its premier pass rusher. As strong as Harrison was, I think people underrated his speed. He made a lot of sacks where he would just set the guy down a little bit coming off the ball with a shake and then he would just burst right around him. The offensive tackle couldn't stay with him. He was so strong that the tackle had to be able to anchor at any time, and that left a lot for the tackle to have to control. That is why he made so many sacks.

This one gave us our first points of the game and also a short field. There were no touchdowns the rest of the game, and we were able to make three Jeff Reed field goals stand up in an 11–10 win that improved our record to 7–3.

It was an unusual game from the standpoint of you can usually look at statistics and get a pretty good feel for how the game was played.

This ended up a one-point game, even though we had 410 total yards, and San Diego had 218. The time of possession was about a 10-minute differential. San Diego passed for 147 yards and could only run for 66 on 3.0 yards per carry. I was really pleased with the job we did against Tomlinson, and as the season went along, teams gave up trying to run on us really.

There were too many good players in the front seven, and they couldn't block them all. You added Polamalu and Clark, who were as good a tacklers at safety as you will ever see, and teams would run a little bit to give the quarterback a rest, but mostly it was counterproductive for them.

Our stars made big plays against San Diego, especially Harrison. In addition to the safety he caused, he intercepted Rivers in the second quarter to give us momentum. He returned it 30 yards to set up a field goal, and we double dipped with another Reed field goal to take an 8–7 lead.

Even though we did not score a touchdown—penalties really hurt us—Roethlisberger turned into Roethlisberger when we needed it most. Our defense gave up a long drive in the fourth quarter but made a stand with our backs to the end zone, holding San Diego to a field goal. Down 10–8 with just more than four minutes to play, Roethlisberger led a methodical 13-play, 72-yard drive. His passing and Willie Parker's running—he gained 38 of his game-high 125 rushing yards—on the drive set up a last-second field goal by Reed that won the game.

It was the 15th time in his young career that Roethlisberger had brought us back from a fourth-quarter deficit for a win and it allowed the Steelers to improve to 13–0 all time against the Chargers in the regular season. It had not been easy, but we had dominated statistics and time of possession and allowed just one touchdown to a really good offense. We had sabotaged ourselves with 13 penalties for 115 yards, but those were mistakes that could be corrected. We had bounced back from a tough loss and beat a pretty good team, coming from behind to do so.

Looking back, this was kind of the turning point of our season. This was our 10th game, and we went into the game at 6–3. We'd win a couple and lose one. Starting with this game, we ended up winning nine of our next 10. This game was the first evidence that this team could do something pretty special. The game featured a game-turning interception by Harrison and a patented Roethlisberger fourth-quarter comeback. We did not know it at the time, but the game was very close to a dress rehearsal for the Super Bowl.

Great Minds Think Alike

The 2008 Pittsburgh Steelers were blessed with two exceptional safeties in Troy Polamalu and Ryan Clark. They got to the NFL in opposite fashion. Polamalu was a first-round pick in 2003, and Clark was an undrafted free agent who played for the Washington Redskins and the New York Giants before signing with the Steelers in 2006. Despite their different paths to the Steelers, each had to earn his way onto the field in Pittsburgh.

Polamalu did not start a game his rookie season before flourishing in 2004—not coincidentally the season when LeBeau took over as the Steelers' defensive coordinator. LeBeau recommended signing Clark after the Steelers lost free safety Chris Hope after the Super Bowl-winning season in 2005. But they still had Tyrone Carter and took Syracuse safety Anthony Smith in the second round of the 2006 NFL Draft. "I had to battle with Tyrone Carter my first camp, and even then Bill Cowher told me Anthony Smith would play," Clark said. "I played so well that he doesn't get to play until Game 12 or 13 when I got hurt. I had to battle with him the next year and I win that in camp as well. But still it was: 'Anthony is going to play a series.' But I think I was always trying to prove myself to people not only in Pittsburgh but everywhere I played."

Clark started the first six games in 2007 but missed the rest of the season after the high altitude in Denver triggered a potentially tragic reaction called splenic infarction due to Clark having a sickle cell trait. He had to be rushed to a hospital and nearly lost his life. He eventually had to have his gall bladder and spleen removed. But the extended time that Clark missed strengthened his hold on the starting free safety job. "When I was cleared to work after my surgeries and battle with sickle cell in January 2008, [defensive backs coach] Ray Horton told me, 'If you are healthy, then you're our guy. We didn't know how much you meant to this team until we didn't have you.' Until that time, I didn't know if I would be strong enough to play again, and they said, 'It's your job,'" Clark said. "I think that's what made 2008 so special for me. The game was almost taken away from me the year before, and [it was] the first year being in Pittsburgh and the NFL, where I felt like I wasn't fighting for my life, where I felt like I belonged. I felt like people wanted me there and to an extent needed me there."

Polamalu and Clark bonded on and off the field and became a dynamic duo. "We spent an awful lot of time together. He's Uncle Troy to my kids, and I'm Uncle Ryan to his kids," Clark said. "His wife is Auntie Theodora, and my wife is Auntie Yonka. That's just who we were as friends. Then as far as football, my job was to give us an extra blade of grass to defend every snap, and my main job was to allow Troy to be as great as he could possibly be and never have to stress about saving the defense. We studied film and we compared notes and talked about how we are going to play certain things and how we are going to tackle certain players."

The two spent so much time together that they developed a sixth sense for each other on the back end of the defense. "A simple look or a point, I knew what he was going to do," Clark said. "We became interchangeable, so Troy could do what he wanted. I needed to know what both safeties did every play. He needed to know what both safeties did every play. If he wanted to do a certain thing based on a certain look, I needed to be able to do whatever the responsibility of the other safety was, and that was just the way we worked in camp...One day I would play right, and he would play left; one day he would play strong, and I would play free. Every day we would do something different that allowed us to be interchangeable. So if we were in a call and he looks at me with his eyes to the right and I'm standing right in front or behind him, I know he's doing whatever the safety to the right is supposed to do in a very Troy way and I'm going to go the left and do whatever that safety is supposed to do in a very Ryan way. That was the way we worked, that was the way we moved together. I think it gave us both the ability to be the best we could be every snap."

It did not escape their teammates how well the two played off each other. "It's very underrated how smart of football players that Troy and especially Ryan Clark are," nose tackle Casey Hampton said. "When you have those two minds together and playing together all those years and being best friends, I think the sky was the limit for those guys. They could do anything. I think they could play the secondary without even talking to each other because of how close they were."

—G.V.B.

11

Hello Again, Cincinnati

I played all 14 of my NFL seasons with the Detroit Lions. My coaching career was a different story. I spent time with six organizations and had two stints with two of them: the Pittsburgh Steelers and Cincinnati Bengals. There's not too much I would have done differently and consider myself incredibly blessed for the experiences I had at all of my coaching stops. If you coach 45 years in the NFL—and that was beyond my wildest dreams when I first broke into coaching with the Philadelphia Eagles—you are going to move around.

That is just the reality of coaching at football's highest level, which made Dick Hoak such a rarity. Hoak was a great running back for the Steelers in the 1960s, a hometown hero who grew up in nearby Jeannette, Pennsylvania. He joined Chuck Noll's staff in 1972 as a running backs coach and stayed in the role until retiring after the 2006 season. I got to know Hoak after I joined Bill Cowher's staff as a defensive backs coach in 1992. Coach Chuck Noll had just retired, and the Steelers hired Cowher to succeed him, making him the youngest coach in the NFL, one who only had to succeed a legend. I did not know Cowher at all. I had spent the previous 12 seasons with the Bengals, and we were let go after the 1991 season—another unfortunate reality in a results-oriented business.

When you don't have a job, you throw your name in there to any place that's turning over. I went to Pittsburgh and talked to the Steelers, and they said they'd let me know. That usually means thanks but no thanks. I waited a pretty good while, and they probably offered the job to a couple of people, and it didn't work out. I had been in that division and knew the teams and knew Pittsburgh's personnel. I joined an excellent staff in Pittsburgh, especially on the defensive side of the ball. Dom Capers was the defensive coordinator, and we had a young linebackers coach by the name of Marvin Lewis. Here is a fun fact about Lewis. His uncle was a doctor in James Farrior's hometown of Ettrick, Virginia, and delivered James Farrior.

Cowher was great to work for as he was a very organized, structured guy. He and Capers were as detailed as any coaches I've been around. Their need to have everything completely defined before they would present it really helped us in "ruling out"—that's a phrase I use—new defenses that we were going to use. Let's face it: my stuff could be off the diving board. A lot of times I said, "We'll just do this, we'll do that," and they both wanted exactness. I think that was a plus for me. I knew where I was going, but it helped me to have to definitely rule out everything for everybody. A lot of times I just had to teach the coaches before I could put it in for the players. When they saw the soundness of it, they were broad-minded enough to embrace it, and we became "Blitzburgh."

The success of those defenses got Capers a head coaching job with the expansion Carolina Panthers in 1995. I took over as defensive coordinator and spent two seasons in that role before returning to Cincinnati as the defensive coordinator and assistant head coach. In 2000 I became a head coach for the first time. It happened during the season after Bruce Coslet resigned. I got the job on a full-time basis after the season and received a two-year contract.

The only thing I didn't enjoy about being a head coach is you don't have time to put together the game plan. You can oversee and have input, but you're dealing with the entire roster, and you've got to keep the engine on the tracks. Every day it's something else, and you don't really have the time to focus on offense, defense, or special teams. Other than that, I loved being a head coach. I thought we were on the right track and making some headway before my contract was not renewed after the 2002 season. Lewis came the next year, and within a couple years, they were in the playoffs, so I didn't leave him a franchise in disarray.

I worked 18 years for the Bengals in two different stints and I always went to the bank with one of their checks that could be cashed. So I've got no complaints. I absolutely have nothing but good feelings for the Brown family, which owns the team. They were people of their word and very trustworthy.

I had a lot of history with Paul Brown, the legendary Cleveland Browns coach who later founded the Bengals. The Browns selected me in the fifth round of the 1959 NFL Draft. Back then training camps were eight weeks long, and I was literally the last player cut from the team, so I had the privilege of being around him for two months. He was so innovative. He was really the first guy to emphasize the passing game in the NFL, the first one to time players in the 40-yard dash. Brown was the first coach to have notebooks, and players drew plays in them after they were put on the chalkboard. His number of firsts are endless.

I got to experience how unique he was as a coach in training camp. The first day of camp, he put in one play: the quarterback sneak. That was all we practiced on offense and defense the first day, and from there all we ever ran in practice was whatever he had installed in the playbook. The rest of practice was individual drills. Since we had two practices a day over eight weeks, the offenses and defenses got installed pretty quickly. This was still the era of single-platoon football, and I had to learn offense and defense since I had also been an offensive halfback at Ohio State. I never played for Brown but coached for him when he owned the Bengals during my first stint in Cincinnati. He was such a fascinating guy, and I had read quite a bit about him.

He had been a quarterback at Massillon High School, which was a national powerhouse, and then at Miami of Ohio, which had always impressed me. What is unique about Brown is that he coached at five different places from Massillon High School to Ohio State to finally the Browns, and throughout his fabled coaching career, he was never *not* the head coach. I made this point to him one time during my favorite Paul Brown story.

In 1984 the USFL expanded, and Pittsburgh was awarded a franchise. The Maulers, as they became, offered me their head coaching job. I was getting along in years a little bit because I had played 14 years and at that time had been coaching around 15 years. Every coach wants to be a head coach, and so I thought, *I better think about this a little bit.* The problem was finding the time.

After the football season was over, we started scouting the top players in our area. As the defensive coordinator, I scouted all the top guys in the draft and traveled to the schools. I worked them out and invested quite a bit of time and travel into that. I was on the road when somebody from the Bengals tried to contact me because they knew that Pittsburgh had offered me this job. When an opportunity does present itself, I think you owe it to everybody to examine it. But after I thought it over, I decided that my job with the Bengals was the better opportunity with the added bonus of not having to move my young family. When I returned after that trip, we had our first big draft meeting, and at the end of the meeting, Coach Brown said, "Dick, will you please stay after I adjourn this meeting? I want to talk to you."

I thought, *Oh, I think I know what this is about.*

After everyone had left, he said, "We've been trying to reach you for over three days, and you didn't call us back." He was very calm and didn't raise his voice—something he never did—but I knew he was pissed.

I said, "Coach, I'll tell you why. I got a job offer and didn't want to answer it until I felt I had checked all the boxes on whether it was a good move or not for me. As soon as I determined that it wasn't, I called you and told you I was going to stay with Cincinnati."

He said, "I don't think it's very professional the way you did it."

I said, "Well, I wouldn't argue that. I've never been a head coach and I had to give this some thought." I went extensively into his coaching career and how he had always been a head coach, and it was an analogy

I was trying to make as to why I took some time to think it over when offered a head coaching position.

He looked at me and said, "I understand that, Dick." Then he said, "Don't ever do it again." He was basically saying: *if you want to work here, when I call you, buddy, you better call my ass back.*

Cincinnati is where I almost won my first Super Bowl, and we could have done it twice if not for Joe Montana and the San Francisco 49ers. We played them twice in the 1980s and came up just short each time. In the second one in 1989, we lost our nose tackle Tim Krumrie to a broken leg early in the game. He had been a first-team All-Pro selection that season, and I always thought he would have come up with a play somewhere that might have made the difference in a close game.

We kicked a field goal to take a 16–13 lead in the fourth quarter, and that is when things got interesting. Our head coach, Sam Wyche, had worked with Bill Walsh, and Walsh had coached him when Wyche was a quarterback for the Bengals. Wyche knew their offense pretty well. He and I had talked quite bit going into the game, and he said, "I'm pretty sure I've got a feel for when Montana is going to go to [Jerry] Rice. I want you to get a coverage that if I get that feeling that there's no way they're going to get it in there."

I said, "Well, Coach, if you rob Peter, you've got to pay Paul. The more I take away from the other coverage, it's going to expose the other guys, but I can give you a coverage that should seal Rice."

He said, "That's what I want. Practice it a little bit because if I come to you in the game when I think it's coming, we can get some miles out of a coverage like that."

I devised this deal where I had a cornerback bumping Rice at the line of scrimmage and I had a safety over the top of him. I also brought down the other safety into the middle of the field, playing the inside of Rice in case he ran a six-cut over the middle. I'm thinking, *There ain't no way they can hit anything on it. But they might hit somebody else because I had to isolate some of the other guys one on one.*

On that drive they were short of midfield, at their own 45-yard line, and it was second down and 20, and I'm thinking, *This is our chance to get the hell out of here.*

But Wyche said: "Dick, this is the play. It's going to go to Rice." I probably would have discussed some other coverage, but this was my boss. So I called it and I crossed my fingers, thinking, *Man, I hope Montana goes to Rice.*

The ball was snapped, and I watched Montana, and his eyes went right to Rice. I said, "He's going to throw to him. We're going to intercept this." Rice ran a six-cut, which is about 12 to 14 yards down the field and in over the middle. I said to myself, *If he throws the ball, he's going to throw it right into that safety that's lurking over there.*

The bump-and-run guy was in pretty good shape on Rice, and there was a guy over top of him. I wasn't worried about him catching anything out there. Montana turned that ball loose, and I'm thinking, *Man, this is perfect. He's throwing that ball right into the middle of these guys.* But the guy driving from the inside out hit the guy driving from the outside in, and the two of those guys wiped out the safety over the top. Rice came up with the catch and ran 35 yards. That's how they got down to our 17-yard line. We had so many guys on Rice that we got in our own way. That's when you know it ain't your day.

Sure enough, Montana finished the drive with a touchdown pass to John Taylor to beat us 20–16. I got that elusive Super Bowl ring in 2005 after I had returned to the Steelers and I thought we were set up really well for more Super Bowl runs. But I faced uncertainty after the 2006 season. Cowher retired, and the Steelers hired Mike Tomlin.

I didn't know Tomlin at all and I didn't know what he was going to do. Our defense was extremely good at that time so I thought I might have a chance to stay. I also knew that Tomlin had been a defensive coordinator when he got hired. I knew he played a 4-3, which I had coached plenty of times, but I didn't know if he would just bring in his own guy. He called me after he got the job and said he was not going to make any changes on defense. I never thought of leaving unless I had to. We were young and pretty damn good. We had won the Super Bowl in 2005 and had a pretty damn good quarterback aboard already, and you ain't looking to leave a quarterback that's won one Super Bowl and is still in his 20s. You figure he might end up getting a couple of more, and we ended up getting to two more Super Bowls.

The first year Tomlin came in, I think we set two hours aside at lunch and I went over anything that I could possibly think anyone would want to know about what we were doing. After we got close to going into training camp, we couldn't meet that long, and I didn't see him as much. He had been a defensive coordinator himself so we hit it off right away. Cowher and I always met on Saturday night—whether it was a home game or an away game—and we always talked things over. I always had a great rapport with both guys. They're both great coaches.

My Pittsburgh and Cincinnati years intersected again a week before Thanksgiving in a Thursday night game at Heinz Field in 2008. It looked like a mismatch on paper. The Bengals came into the game 1–8–1 and without their No. 1 wide receiver, Chad Johnson, who had been suspended. They were missing several offensive linemen, too. We seemed to have every advantage going into the game, but just like in our first meeting, this game showed how hard it is to win in the NFL. Again using a quick, short passing game to neutralize our pass rush, Cincinnati put together a nice drive in the first quarter. Ryan Fitzpatrick completed six-of-seven passes and capped an 11-play drive with a 10-yard touchdown pass to Glenn Holt.

Our offense got going in the second quarter, and we tied the game after Ben Roethlisberger threw a three-yard touchdown pass to Heath

Miller. Our starting tight end had missed the previous two games with an ankle injury, and he was such a big part of our offense.

We added another field goal in the quarter to take a 10–7 lead into halftime, a score that was much closer than most probably expected between two teams that were going in opposite directions. The Bengals played us tough that night, but Roethlisberger and our defense were too much for them. Take away Cincinnati's only touchdown drive, and it managed just 146 yards of total offense. We also made a key defensive stop before the end of the first half after a fumble set up Cincinnati at our 31-yard line. Roethlisberger threw for 243 yards, and his eight-yard touchdown run with just more than two minutes left in the game sealed the 27–10 victory. Troy Polamalu ended a last-gasp Cincinnati drive with his fourth interception of the season.

One unique aspect from that game is we got a key sack from cornerback Fernando Bryant, whom we had signed off the street less than two weeks earlier. In a cool twist of fate, I had coached his father, James Griffin, in Cincinnati. He was one of three Steelers players in that game whose fathers I had coached while with the Bengals. The other two were Andre Frazier, a special teams standout and the son of Guy Frazier, and starting left tackle Max Starks, whose father was former Bengals defensive end Ross Browner. All of them were solid players and good kids—and reminders that I had been coaching for quite a few years in the National Football League.

The season sweep of the Bengals had not been as easy as the final scores indicated, but we were 8–3 with a mini-break before one of our biggest games of the season. We were headed to New England on Thanksgiving weekend, where Tom Brady and the Patriots had been anything but hospitable to us a year earlier.

Consistency and Longevity

The National Football League has been around for 104 years. That makes the story of two former Pittsburgh Steelers assistant coaches remarkable. Dick Hoak, who retired from coaching in 2007, spent 45 years with the Steelers as a player and running backs coach. Dick LeBeau, who turned 86 years old on September 9, 2023, retired from coaching in 2018 after serving as defensive coordinator for the Tennessee Titans for two seasons.

LeBeau joined the Titans after a second stint as defensive coordinator for the Steelers for 11 seasons (2004–2014). Overall, he spent 13 seasons as defensive coordinator for the Steelers, and the zone blitz architect's accomplishments during those 13 seasons are staggering: 10 top-five defensive rankings, five seasons as the league's No. 1 defense, four AFC championships, two Super Bowl wins, and nine playoff appearances.

Hoak and LeBeau had a combined 104 years in the NFL as players and coaches, longevity that produced mutual respect. "Dick Hoak spent 45 years with one organization," LeBeau marveled. "That will probably never happen again."

Hoak starred at Jeannette High School, which is about 30 miles east of Pittsburgh, and Penn State before the Steelers selected him in the seventh round of the 1961 NFL Draft. "I'm happy it happened the way it did," Hoak said. "This is my home, and one of the things I'm very happy with is I had three kids and I never had to move them all around the country. I had opportunities to go some places as a coordinator, but I turned them down. I'm very appreciative of the Rooneys and what they did for me and to Coach [Chuck] Noll and Coach [Bill] Cowher for keeping me there."

In a profession where assistant coaches are like nomads, going from one team to another and rarely survive a coaching change, Hoak remained with the same organization for five decades as a player and then a position coach. He worked under the only three head coaches the Steelers have had since 1969: Noll, Cowher, and Mike Tomlin.

That stability is a big reason why the Steelers have won six Super Bowls since the mid-1970s. "You keep your same system," Hoak said. "You don't change things around; the players don't have to learn a different offense every year. You stay with the system and, when you find something that works, you keep doing it."

That sounds like the ageless LeBeau's coaching career in a nutshell. "I'm amazed that he until recently was still going strong," Hoak said. "I'm not amazed that he did it because I knew he could do it. Dick always took care of himself and he's always in great shape. The physical part you can do that, but what is amazing is the mental part of it. The hours you have to put in, it's not an easy job. You spend a lot of hours, and people think when the season's over, you don't do anything until the next season, but you still work a lot of hours during the day. He loved it and had the energy level."

LeBeau, who has seen it all, said the game fundamentally remains the same. "I've seen a lot of changes, but the basic ingredient in football is not going to change," he said. "Somebody is carrying the ball, and you've got to find him and get him on the ground, and if you are the offensive guy, you've got to protect him and get him across that goal line. That can never change. So it's always going to be blocking, tackling, and execution. The ability to throw and catch has increased more, but it's still football, and I don't think that's going to change."

LeBeau worked on a year-to-year basis, but he never lost his zest for the game. "I've always loved coaching and I've loved teaching and I really didn't pay any attention to age," LeBeau said. "Age is really just a number, and chronological age and physiological age are just two different things. My parents and my ancestors and the good Lord gave me some good genes, and I don't intend to abuse 'em any sooner than I have to. I was going to get as many miles out of them as I can and just go to work."

In 2017 the Steelers introduced the inaugural class of the team's Hall of Honor. Twenty-seven of the team's most famous names were in that first class, including Hoak. "It meant a lot to be in there with some of the great players who played this game," said Hoak, who had 5,017 rushing and receiving yards and 33 touchdowns while playing for the Steelers from 1961 to 1970. "It's nice that the Steelers have done that. I used to go to [other] stadiums and I'd see they had a ring of honor, and the Steelers never had it. I thought it was a great idea and I'm very honored to have been selected in the first class."

—G.V.B.

12

Redemption in New England

I played on some great teams with the Detroit Lions. Our secondary was filled with future Pro Football Hall of Famers like Dick "Night Train" Lane, Yale Lary, and Lem Barney. A fellow by the name of LeBeau also made it to Canton, Ohio.

Joe Schmidt was a larger-than-life character and also one of the greatest middle linebackers in NFL history. He was built like a refrigerator. He was about four-feet wide in the shoulders and about one-and-a-half-feet wide at the hip and could run and also had great timing. He was a great hitter, great player. He could get off in pass coverage and intercept the ball. One of my favorite stories from my playing days stars Schmidt. We'd be in the huddle, and he'd be right in the middle of it calling the defense. I was just a young kid, and Lary was the safety on my side. He would always get in the huddle and say "Wide-side right!" That was before they changed the hashmarks. There was actually a wide and short side of the field.

One game we gave up about a 14-play drive and we didn't give up too many of those because we had a hell of a defense. They just kept converting first downs and moving the ball. On that drive the ball was on the left hash most of the time. I was on the right side and I'd get in the huddle and say, "Wide-side right" because that's what Lary always did when he was the safety on that side of the field before Schmidt had started getting his thought process to call the defense. It got to around play No. 10, and they were on about our 10-yard line. The officials were a foot away because there was nowhere to go, and we're lined in the end zone. I stepped in and said, "Wide-side, right."

Schmidt said, "Will you shut the hell up with that wide-side right shit? I know where the wide side is!"

I said, "Well, the hell with you, Schmidt!" The official's eyes got a little bit wider. He thought we were going to fight.

The postscript to the story is that they didn't score, and Schmidt and I made up as soon as we got off the field. I don't know if I ever said, "Wide-side right" again.

Schmidt was our captain every year and a great one. He became our head coach later on and was a great coach. The one thing the Lions teams I played on did not have was good timing. From my rookie season in 1959 until 1969, there weren't really any playoffs. We had to win our conference or later our division to make it to the postseason. We were second in our conference a bunch of times when only the winner in each conference played in the NFL Championship Game. The runner-up teams in each conference played in a game that we called the Toilet Bowl. They took the money from that runner-up bowl—I think the owners matched it—to fund the first NFL pension for the players. We played in it a handful of times, and the players took it seriously. We got like $1,500 if we won and $1,100 if we lost. We were happy to have it. A $400 difference between winning and losing was significant back then.

We never were quite able to break through when I played for the Lions, and the Pittsburgh Steelers had experienced something similar while trying to win that elusive fifth Super Bowl title. We had gotten to the Super Bowl in 1995 but lost to the Dallas Cowboys. And in the 2000s, the emergence of Tom Brady turned the New England Patriots into a dynasty or as close to one as there could be in an era of the salary cap and unfettered free agency. They had become a nemesis of the Steelers, beating them in the 2001 and 2004 AFC Championship Games. The latter snapped a 15-game winning streak during Ben Roethlisberger's rookie season.

Brady was 5–1 against the Steelers and in 2007 he dominated us, throwing for 399 yards and four scores in a 34–13 win. We did not have Troy Polamalu or Ryan Clark for that game, and it showed. I think that's probably the worst game we ever played defensively.

As competitors we would have loved another crack at Brady in 2008, but he had been sidelined for the season by a torn ACL. Even with Brady out, this game loomed as a measuring stick for us. The Patriots still had Bill Belichick on the sidelines and players like Randy Moss, who was as good as any wide receiver who ever played, especially on deep balls. We had seen that the previous season when he caught seven passes for 135 yards and two touchdowns.

Matt Cassel had stepped in at quarterback and done a pretty good Brady impression. He had thrown for more than 400 yards in each of New England's previous two games and six total touchdowns with one interception. Everybody was going out of their mind over this guy. Cassel had roomed with Polamalu at Southern Cal, but I never talked to players about stuff like that when putting together a defensive game plan. I just studied a lot of film on the quarterbacks we were playing against. If a guy played for an opposing coach, I might on occasion ask if he had ever said anything about what he liked to do against us.

The weather for the late-afternoon game was probably about as good as you'd expect for late November in New England. It was 34 degrees at kickoff, but it had been misting all day. We won the toss and took the ball first in part because of the weather and trying to have the ball while the day was as dry as it was going to get.

The game initially looked like a continuation of the disaster that had taken place the previous year at Gillette Stadium. A penalty and fumble on the opening kickoff had our offense starting on its 10-yard line. Four plays later Mike Vrabel intercepted a pass and gave New England the ball at our 15-yard line. On second down the Patriots hit a pass down to our 4-yard line and then they ran it in for a touchdown. So it was 7–0, and the paint wasn't even dry on the seats yet.

We went three-and-out, and then James Farrior and Aaron Smith made a play when we really needed one. The Patriots were at midfield after a 27-yard catch by Moss when Farrior and Smith sacked Cassel on third down, forcing a punt. Roethlisberger and the offense got something going, starting with a 21-yard pass play to Heath Miller. Completions of 15 and 16 yards to Nate Washington helped us get to the Patriots' 2-yard line, but on third and 1, New England stuffed running back Gary Russell for no gain. We took the points to make the score 7–3.

After New England kicked a short field goal, Roethlisberger and Mewelde Moore led our first touchdown drive of the game. Willie Parker had been bothered by a knee injury, so they were monitoring his carries, and Moore ran really well. Our intention when we signed Moore was for him to be a third-down back, but when Parker got hurt, he ended up carrying the brunt of the load because Rashard Mendenhall had broken his clavicle earlier in the year against the Baltimore Ravens.

Moore was really a stabilizing force at running back for us. He had 32 rushing and receiving yards on the drive that Roethlisberger capped with a 19-yard touchdown pass to Santonio Holmes. I don't know if there was a busted coverage, but Holmes was all by himself in the end zone. His touchdown tied the game at 10, and it remained that way going into halftime.

It was anybody's game, but we owned the third quarter that season. New England was our 12th game, and we had given up a total of *nine* points in the third quarter. That is a crazy statistic for the modern era of football.

We did not give up any points in the third *or* fourth quarter on this day and dominated the second half. Casey Hampton really got it rolling. Aided by a pass interference call, New England drove inside our territory on the opening possession of the second half. On second and 1 from the 31-yard line, Hampton made one of the biggest plays of the game while recording his first sack of the season. He took the center and the guard and just indented the line of scrimmage on a play-action pass. When Cassel came out of the fake, Hampton was six inches from him. He just engulfed the whole line of scrimmage and took down Cassel. It was one of the better plays that I've seen a defensive lineman make.

Hampton was kind of the unsung hero of the whole defense. The nose tackle doesn't get involved in many splash plays. His job oftentimes is to occupy two or three blockers, which the good ones often do, and Hampton was one of the best. It's a pretty selfless person who will play the position because you're just working your tail off every down and you're never going to be the Homecoming king, but great players usually make exceptional plays in the situation when your team needs it the most. It was a huge time in the game as it was tied up, and they were moving the ball. After Hampton sacked Cassel, we defended the third down, and they had to punt.

After a Jeff Reed field goal midway through the third quarter, the game tilted. His kickoff bounced off Matthew Slater's shoulder pads and bounced sideways. Our coverage team did a great job of knocking him out of the way so he could not recover the loose ball, and Keyaron Fox pounced on it at the 8-yard line. On our second play, Roethlisberger threw an 11-yard touchdown pass to Hines Ward, and that opened the floodgates. After the ensuing kickoff, James Harrison got a sack fumble on second down, and LaMarr Woodley recovered the fumble. That one-two punch was always a joy to watch. That was our second takeaway in two minutes, and we got the ball on the New England 26-yard line. We had to settle for field goal, but it was 23–10.

After the field goal, Polamalu almost got another pick. It was a jump ball between him and the receiver, and on the next snap, we had an unnecessary roughness penalty, which gave them their biggest gain of the second half. We got them to third down, and Harrison, using the same kind of speed move, got another sack fumble. It looked like a replay of the play we just had five minutes earlier. This one was recovered by Farrior, and it led to another field goal.

We had taken the ball away on New England's final four possessions of the game. The last one put the game away when Lawrence Timmons picked off a flat pass and returned it 85 yards before getting tackled at the 1-yard line. We had a fun time with him in the meeting later that week when we reviewed film of the game. He was flying after the interception, and by the time he got down to about the 20-yard line, it was like someone threw a piano on his back. He was staggering in there, and they barely got him down at the 1-yard line.

Russell punched it in from there, punctuating a 33–10 win. I could not have been more pleased with the defense, especially in the second half. The guys, though, did give me something to hold their attention as New England ran for 122 yards and averaged 6.1 yards per carry. No one had come close to that all season, and we needed to fix that, which we would.

We forced five turnovers, and the statistic that pleased me most was holding New England to one third-down conversion on 13 attempts. That's fairy-tale stuff for the NFL. The biggest takeaway from that game was how we made timely plays on both sides of the ball. In key situations in the game, Hampton made a great sack, and then Roethlisberger hit Ward to give us some breathing room, turning a three-point lead into a 10-point lead. The leaders of our team came through, and that was the trademark of the 2008 team. The tightest part of the year, the tightest part of the game, our guys came up with the plays. And they were far from finished making them.

Riding with Night Train

Dick LeBeau played 14 seasons with the Detroit Lions and teamed with future Pro Football Hall of Famers Dick "Night Train" Lane, Yale Lary, and Lem Barney as part of a Detroit secondary that was one of the most feared in the NFL. The "wildest" game that LeBeau ever played in while with the Lions also produced one of LeBeau's favorite Lane stories.

It came on December 4, 1960, at Memorial Stadium in Baltimore in a game that featured great players and clutch plays. After the Lions kicked a field goal in the fourth quarter to take a 13–8 lead, Baltimore Colts quarterback Johnny Unitas led his team down the field. He threw a 38-yard touchdown pass to Lenny Moore with 14 seconds left to play. Moore made the catch despite being blanketed by Lane. "Night Train was in pretty good shape on it, and they both went up for the ball, and it was an absolute perfect pass and it just dropped over Night Train's outstretched arms into the outstretched arms of Moore, and the two of them fell into the end zone," LeBeau recalled. "The stadium was packed, and fans were ringed around the field. When Moore came down with the ball, all the fans flooded into the end zone and picked up Moore and carried him off the field. It was a mass of humanity and it took the officials 10 minutes to get everybody off the field. They had to kick the extra point and kick off to us. The game wasn't over."

Indeed, Lions quarterback Earl Morrall connected with Jim Gibbons on the final play, and Gibbons broke free for a 65-yard touchdown and 19–15 Lions win. The two teams scored two touchdowns in the final 14 seconds. "It was the wildest game I was ever involved in." LeBeau said. "It was the most thrilling finish to a football game I'd ever seen. Everybody was going crazy in the locker room. I saw Night Train and I walked over to him and said, 'On that play where Moore caught that ball. I was sincerely afraid for you.' I mean it was a dangerous situation."

His response was classic Night Train. He said that the fans, whom LeBeau had feared might trample him, had saved his life. "You mean almost took your life," LeBeau said.

Lane then explained to LeBeau how they helped him in a way. "I dove for the ball, and Moore dove for it. I thought I had it, and it just went over my fingertips, and I saw it go into Moore's arms, and we hit the ground, and I saw him roll over. I realized that he had caught the ball in the last few seconds of the game. I was in a state of shock. Then all those people started kicking me and brought me back to my senses."

"I have a million Night Train stories," LeBeau said. "He was a character."

Another favorite story of LeBeau's happened during Lions' training camp in 1967. A reporter asked Lane his thoughts on Barney, who had just joined the team as a second-round draft pick out of Jackson State. "Lem was pretty exciting and the talk of the training camp," LeBeau said. "They asked Train what he thought about this young rookie. Night Train said, 'Well, he's got great balance, he's athletic, he's so fast. His ball skills are A 1. When I watch him, sometimes I think I'm watching myself.' That was classic Night Train."

—G.V.B.

13
Townsend Steps Up against Lone-Star Rival

We were rolling along pretty good after beating the Patriots in New England. Holding that offense—even without Tom Brady—scoreless in the second half was something, and it helped us break open the game. It was the third straight game that our opponent had only scored 10 points. We had still yet to give up more than 300 total yards in a game. By now it was pretty clear that we had a special defense—even if the focus inside our facility remained on our next opponent, not posterity.

Fans saw greatness from our defense on a weekly basis, but they were not privy to behind-the-scenes work that defined this defense every bit as much as one of Troy Polamalu's highlight-reel plays, the relentlessness of our pass rush, and the consistency of our players, starting with James Farrior. As talented as this group was—and a handful of our reserves could have been starters elsewhere—boy, did these guys put in the work. In a typical week, we spent Mondays reviewing Sunday's game. Coaches graded film, and then we walked through some stuff. We went over errors made and things players wished they had done better. With this group those walkthroughs did not last very long. The players were off on Tuesdays—standard for most, if not all, teams in the league. Coaches hunkered down in the facility, putting together the game plan for the next opponent.

Wednesdays represented the start of the next work week for the players. It was probably their longest day of the week. We met as a defense to install the defense, and to the outsider, it would have seemed rather tedious, pedantic even. But what do they say? The devil is in the details, and in the NFL, even the most minute details can be the difference between winning and losing. That is what made those Wednesday meetings with this group so special. When we were behind closed doors, you could have heard a pin drop. Every coach got the utmost attention to their section of the game plan. I kicked off the meeting, and each coach took a portion of the scouting report. I'd just look around, and it was awesome to see the preparation the guys put in and the focus that they had. They would take notes and comment to one another quickly and then focus on the information that was coming in. They were developing trust with one another. They could see how hard each person was working.

Any good defense has the complete trust of everyone in the huddle. If you don't have that, it's going to break down at some point because 11 men have to be doing their job the majority of the time to be successful. There are just too many good athletes on the other side of the ball. When I was showing the game film on Mondays, I'd spotlight the guys hustling, making plays, and supporting everything we were preaching for team defense. If it was really a play that I liked, if it was making a point I wanted to make, I might run it back 12 times. I wanted everyone to see how hard that was to do and the effort that it took. They all were good enough that at one time or another they were the featured guy. They were close and they believed in each other.

That—and the players' meticulous preparation—showed up time and time again. It did in a big way in our game against the Dallas Cowboys on the first Sunday in December. The Pittsburgh Steelers and Cowboys have a lot of history, of course. They seemed to be inextricably linked in the 1970s, winning titles and playing in classic Super Bowls that made the Steelers a dynasty.

I have my own history with Dallas, dating back to my playing days. We came in together in some ways. My first NFL season preceded Dallas joining the league as an expansion franchise by one year. Dallas struggled at first, going winless its first season under a young, first-time NFL head coach by the name of Tom Landry. That's the way it is with expansion teams. It's almost like they have to go through a probationary period, taking their lumps while trying to claw their way up from the bottom.

After paying its dues, Dallas broke through in a big way. It made the NFL Championship Game in 1966 and 1967. From then on, the Cowboys always seemed to be in the running for championships. They were always respected and almost always good. Any time they're on your schedule, it's a game you start working on in the summer before you go to camp.

Actually, the first time the Detroit Lions teams that I played on made the playoffs, we played Dallas in the Cotton Bowl in 1970, the day after Christmas. I drew the unenviable assignment of covering Cowboys wide receiver Bob Hayes for much of that game as he usually lined up on my side of the field. His nickname was "Bullet" for good reason. He had been a world-class sprinter, winning a pair of gold medals at the 1964 Olympics. There still weren't many people on the planet faster than Hayes when we played Dallas.

The first thing you didn't want to do was get in a foot race with him. If nobody else could beat him, it was unlikely you were going to. Another thing about Hayes was he was so powerful. When he took off, the dirt looked like a rooster tail on a hydroplaned racing boat. It just flew behind him. Whenever I saw that dirt fly, I got the hell out of there. He was taking off. We stopped them pretty good that game. Unfortunately, it was a tough day for our offense, too, and Dallas beat us 5–0. (Yes, that is not a misprint.) Neither offense did much, resulting in what is only one of three 5–0 outcomes in the long history of the NFL.

While planning for Dallas in 2008 in a crucial game for each team, I knew the Cowboys did not have anyone as fast as "Bullet Bob" in his prime, but they were plenty good on offense. Tony Romo came into the game as the top-rated quarterback in the league. Dallas had a great tight end in Jason Witten, who played forever. He and Romo were joined at the hip, and Witten was far from his only weapon. Terrell Owens was a great wide receiver. Roy Williams was another tall wide receiver. Dallas did not have its top running back, Marion Barber, who was out with an injury. It also did not have weather on its side for an air-it-out game. It was a late afternoon kickoff and very windy. It was 20 degrees but eight degrees with the windchill. It was a good day to be hosting Dallas since a Texas team like that was a bit less accustomed to playing in the cold. Its record was 8–4; we were 9–3. It was a must-have game for both teams. We were in a dogfight with the Baltimore Ravens for our division, and they were in one with the New York Giants in the NFC East.

Polamalu entered the game with a league-leading five interceptions and he made a pick near midfield on the first series of the game. We couldn't turn it into points as we missed a 45-yard field goal. Heinz Field is a particularly tough place to kick when it is windy, and this day was no different. Dallas responded with a drive that reached our 35-yard line. Facing a fourth and inches, the Cowboys went for it, and we stuffed fullback Deon Anderson for no gain. On short-yardage and goal-line situations, our guys were unbelievable. The guys up front couldn't be blocked, and Polamalu was usually sticking his nose right in where the ball was going.

At the end of the first quarter, it was scoreless. We turned the ball over at midfield, and they again got down to our 35-yard line. On fourth and 2, we stopped them again. Romo had something wrong with his non-throwing hand. He had been wearing a glove but had taken it off for this game. The wind, the cold, and the injury affected him. The defense had an impact on him also, and he only posted a 44.9 quarterback rating for the game—well below his average. That speaks to the level of defense that the guys were playing that day. One of the TV commentators said, "You can't name a stat that they don't lead the league in." So we were starting to get some notice from the numbers we were throwing up there.

A stop on fourth and short to me is like a turnover because there are no points, and the offense doesn't gain field position from a punt. It's not in the statistics, but it was always on my stat chart that I talked to the players about. After an interception to start the game and two fourth-down stops, we came up with another takeaway early in the second quarter.

We ran a fire-zone blitz on third down on the Cowboys' fourth possession and got a sack fumble. This was yet another instance of our depth showing up. We had signed defensive end Travis Kirschke as a free agent in 2004, and he proved to be a great addition. He started six games for us in 2008 because of injuries to Brett Keisel and did an excellent job. Keisel did not play against the Cowboys because of a knee injury, and Kirschke had one of his better games. He recovered a fumble after James Harrison made a good pass rush move and sacked Romo. It was Harrison's 15th sack of the season. It was also his 13th forced fumble over a 20-game stretch. That was extraordinary.

We fumbled it right back to the Cowboys, and that was the story of the first half. We just could not get anything going. We only had 89 yards of total offense at halftime. Dallas had 134, but our defense had two fourth-down stops and three takeaways. The third one set up the first points of the game, a field goal after Ike Taylor picked off a Romo pass deep in Cowboys' territory. It was our ninth takeaway in four quarters. Dallas tied the game right before the half with a field goal of its own.

Dallas put together its best drive of the game early in the third quarter, one that resulted in the first touchdown for either team. We had them at third and 3 on their own 40-yard line when they gashed us with a draw play. That was one of those play calls I'd like to have back. They hit it for 22 yards with Tashard Choice, the running back who was playing for the injured Barber. When calling a defense on third and 3, you want to be as conservative as possible. But in a game in which you're tied up and it's obviously going to be a fourth-quarter game between two good defenses, I think you just want to let the players decide the game. I thought they would throw the ball and called a little bit of an unbalanced defense. It didn't work because they hit that draw play, which allowed them to get the drive started. We had been forcing a bunch of three-and-outs to that point. That was only the third run of more than 20 yards that we had given up that season. I wss thinking on the sidelines it probably wasn't the players' fault.

To this point we had allowed no touchdowns in the third quarter; we ended up leading the league in that. Romo changed that, throwing a 12-yard touchdown pass to Owens. The Cowboys had the wind in the third quarter, and that was the best they moved the ball all game. I was thinking on the sidelines that if we get through the quarter and get the wind behind us—that is usually a huge factor in close games—that we would be okay.

The Cowboys and Choice had other ideas. After we punted he made another big play. He broke a couple of tackles after taking a check-down pass for 50 yards before being tackled at our 10-yard line. With the way Dallas' defense was playing and the weather, it made the situation dire. We needed a stop in the worst way and got it. On third down from the 7-yard line, I called a max blitz, and Farrior made a huge sack. Dallas kicked a field goal to make the score 13–3.

That led to a play that was a forerunner of things to come. We were facing a third and 16 on our own 20-yard line. I was on the sidelines and said, "Well, I know our offense is going to get going." Ben Roethlisberger and Santonio Holmes provided the spark we desperately needed, hooking up on a go route for 47 yards. That play picked everybody up on the sidelines. When you needed Roethlisberger the most, he showed up. That was kind of a theme of the season, too. We didn't score after Dallas made a goal-line stand, but that play flipped the field position.

With nine minutes to play, Dallas faced a third and 6; it was a must-stop situation. We had to get the ball back for the offense, and Polamalu made a fantastic play. He went flying through two or three different blockers and made the cleanest, sharpest tackle on Choice for a one-yard loss to force the punt. That was his ninth tackle of the game, and none was bigger than that. We were running out of time and needed to get the ball back.

Holmes made another big play, returning the punt 35 yards to the Cowboys' 25-yard line. That set up a Jeff Reed field goal that made the score 13–6. The kick hit the right goal post before going through the uprights, so someone was liking us, and things were starting to come our way. We needed another stop after Dallas got good field position with the clock working against us. Kirschke made a great sack on second down, highlighting the three-and-out we forced.

Roethlisberger went to work after Dallas punted. He completed passes of 14, 21, and 16 yards to Nate Washington, who emerged as a deep threat as the season progressed. That put us at Dallas' 6-yard line with just more than two minutes to play. Dallas went max blitz on first down, and Roethlisberger hit Heath Miller, a pretty common refrain in the Steelers offense for a long time, for a touchdown. That tied the game up with two minutes to play. Our kickoff coverage team stopped Dallas on the 15-yard line. They ran the ball on first down and got two yards. We took a timeout with 1:51 to play. If we got off the field, we figured we had a pretty good chance to win the game.

That is when the rapt attention that the players showed in our Wednesday meetings came to the forefront. I had talked to our guys all week that when the Cowboys needed a play, Romo was probably going to look at Witten first. Deshea Townsend, our nickel cornerback, felt like the defense had a pretty good read on when Witten was going to do a certain move. I adjusted him and Polamalu ever so slightly in a defense we always used in practice and had ready in case we needed it in a game. Townsend thought he could get to Witten if he had the free pass to do it. I said, "We'll give them this look, and you and Troy make this adjustment. If he goes to Witten, I think you'll have a good chance to get the ball."

It was pretty easy to improvise it, and that was another plus of that group of guys. Because we had been together and in the same system with the same coaching, we could do that. A rule of thumb for me is I wouldn't call anything in a game that we hadn't at least walked through in practice. But situations like this would come up in a game. To take advantage of what the opponent was doing, you had to change a couple of things. I just figured out a way we could do it with Townsend and Polamalu the only ones involved in the adjustment, and everybody else just played a straight zone.

I don't know whether it confused Romo or Witten, but the ball was four or five yards away from Witten, and Polamalu and Townsend executed their parts perfectly. I don't know if Witten saw the look and changed his route, or whether Romo saw the different look and just let it go, but Townsend read it just like he thought he could, and I was lucky enough to get the thing called at the right time. Townsend intercepted it and ran it in for a touchdown. The guys that I had—Ryan Clark, Polamalu, Townsend, Taylor, Larry Foote, Farrior, Harrison, and LaMarr Woodley—were so comfortable with the defense that you could make chess moves a little bit and make adjustments like that. It was their idea in the first place. Townsend thought he could get it and he got it.

His touchdown brought us all the way back from a 10-point, second-half deficit. It foreshadowed another pick-six, one that would define this defense more than any other play. Not that we had much time to celebrate our 10th win of the season. A trip to Baltimore awaited us. It would be another back-alley brawl, and this one had huge AFC North and playoff implications.

Best Friends Forever

One handshake. One look in the eyes. That is all it took for Bill Priatko's life to change forever.

He and Dick LeBeau first met when they roomed together at Cleveland Browns' training camp in 1959. Thirteen United States presidential administrations later, they remain the best of friends. "It didn't take long from that meeting to see what a genuine, humble guy he was," Priatko said.

Get the two together, and they are history coming to life—and not just the NFL. One day they were having lunch at Grand View Golf Course in the North Braddock section of Pittsburgh. The area is famous as a flashpoint for the French and Indian War, and LeBeau is a history buff. "He looked down at the Monongahela River," Priatko recalled, "and he said, 'That's where General Braddock came across with his troops.'"

Priatko said LeBeau knows everything about the war, but he drew a quizzical look from his pal when he said the area wasn't where the fiercest fighting ever took place. Priatko said that happened at nearby North Braddock Scott High School on Friday nights. Priatko had starred there before playing at Pitt and in the NFL. The two got a good laugh out of that.

An easy give and take defines their friendship, and the two can downright act like teenagers around each other. When LeBeau was head coach of the Cincinnati Bengals in the early 2000s, Priatko visited him at training camp. After a night practice, they retired to LeBeau's room where a film projector and box of Snickers bars were waiting for them. They stayed up until four in the morning. "All we did was drink Pepsi and eat Snickers bars while we were going over his defenses on the wall," Priatko said with a laugh.

They presumably ate much healthier during LeBeau's two coaching stints with the Pittsburgh Steelers. Priatko, who had played for the Steelers, watched practice every Friday at team headquarters. Afterward, he and LeBeau ate lunch together in the Steelers' cafeteria. It became such a tradition that when Priatko had to go on a different day one week, Steelers kicker Shaun Suisham asked him, "Hey, Bill, what are you doing down here? It's Thursday."

Before Priatko would leave those Friday get-togethers, LeBeau would often remind him to call that night with scores from the high school games. LeBeau has always loved the game at that level and respected the coaches, stemming from how much he revered his high school coach, Jim Bowlus, when he played at London High School. "He knew about Woodland Hills and Upper St. Clair and Clairton and Aliquippa, all those teams," Priatko said. "He was really into high school football in Western Pennsylvania."

One story that Priatko will never forget happened when he attended a Western Pennsylvania Hall of Fame induction ceremony for Joe Walton. He was with Joe Mucci, a legendary Western Pennsylvania high school coach, when they spotted former Washington Redskins quarterback Joe Theismann. They approached Theismann, who had been coached by Walton while playing for the Redskins. Mucci said he was friends with Theismann's high school coach, and the three started talking. Somehow LeBeau's name came up. "He looked at Joe Mucci and me and said, 'Let me tell you something about Coach LeBeau. He is the best defensive coordinator in the game of football. Not just the NFL,'" Priatko recalled. "I smiled and said, 'Joe, I happen to agree with you.'"

The ties between LeBeau and Priatko run so deep that it is not uncommon for LeBeau to call and sing to Priatko and his children when one of them has a birthday. The morning after LeBeau got inducted into the Pro Football Hall of Fame in 2010, Priatko and two of his children, Debbie and Dan, were at a table with the LeBeaus during a Hall of Fame breakfast. Dan is a West Point graduate and Army Ranger who suffered catastrophic injuries in a car accident right before his first deployment.

Doctors did not initially think he would survive, but Dan has long been an inspiration for battling back and never complaining after the injuries ended his military career, which may have ended with him becoming a general. That morning LeBeau and his wife, Nancy, presented a Hall of Fame football to Dan. It had been signed by everyone who had been inducted the night before, and they insisted he keep it. "I never forgot that," Bill Priatko said. "They are always so kind to our family."

—S.B.

14

Another Steelers–Ravens Classic

The games do not get much bigger than when the Pittsburgh Steelers and Baltimore Ravens play against each other late in the season. Our December 14 game in Baltimore had been scheduled for Sunday night so it would be nationally televised. We were really playing well, having won four in a row to reach 10–3. We controlled our own destiny in the AFC. If we won out, we would have home-field advantage in the playoffs. Not that we could think about that since the Ravens still stood in our way of winning the AFC North.

It was John Harbaugh's first year coaching and quarterback Joe Flacco's first year playing, but they had surprised some people, going 9–4, and with a win, they would split the season series and have the same record as us. Like us, they were a complete defense, so we knew points would be at a premium.

The fanfare that preceded the game provided a stark contrast to when I arrived in Baltimore—at the start of my playing career in 1959—in the city where I thought I might put down some roots. I was drafted by the Cleveland Browns that year, and it was a different time in so many ways, including roster sizes. NFL teams only had 31 players then. Most only carried five defensive backs. I made it to the end of training camp but got cut the Tuesday before the start of the regular season. I went home and hoped somebody would claim me. In those days they had what they called taxi squads. By the time I was coming into the league, they were paying the taxi squad enough so that players on it didn't have to get another job. After I was cut, Baltimore—they were the Colts back then—called and wanted me to be on the taxi squad. The Colts were the reigning world champions, but I didn't know anyone there.

The Detroit Lions had also called me about joining their taxi squad, and I called Howard "Hopalong" Cassady. He had been an All-American and Heisman Trophy winner at Ohio State and was a senior when I was a freshman in Columbus. When I was at Ohio State, there was a tradition that at the end of the season graduating seniors would leave their locker to one of the freshmen. Cassady left his to me, which was a great honor, and he wrote a little inspirational message that he left in the locker for me.

I knew him pretty well, and he was playing for the Lions when I was considering the two taxi squad offers. I called him to ask him about the defensive back situation in Detroit, and he said the Lions were really good there. Cassady asked, "What's the other team?" I said Baltimore, and he said, "They are the world champs."

I said, "I know, but I also know Detroit is a lot closer to my home in London, Ohio."

He said, "In all honesty, we've got a pretty good young secondary." That settled it for me. I figured if I was going to be on a taxi squad, I might as well go to the world champs.

I flew to Baltimore, and the Colts happened to be opening the regular season at home against the Lions. I got picked up in the owner's limousine and driven to a little neighborhood near Memorial Stadium. The Colts had given me some advance money, and I rented a room. I practiced with them the next day, which was a Thursday, and it was the last padded practice before the game. They had told me they would pay me $700 a week, but I was still waiting for someone to say something to me about signing a contract. I was given a sideline pass for the game, and during pregame warm-ups, Cassady saw me and said, "Dick, why didn't you come to Detroit?"

I said, "You told me not to come."

He said, "I didn't know that they wanted you, and you got me in trouble." He asked if I had signed anything, and I said no. He said, "Will you come in and talk to the head coach, George Wilson, and the football operations manager after the game?" I said I would.

Detroit led Baltimore the whole game, but Johnny Unitas did his thing, and on the last drive, he took the Colts down the field. They scored a touchdown and won the game by four points. I walked over to the Lions' dressing room and I met with Wilson. He said, "We want you. What are they paying you?" I told him $700 a week, and he said, "We'll give you $750."

I had one more thing left to do before leaving Baltimore. Even though the Colts had yet to sign me to a contract, they had given me around $400 for expenses. I had hardly spent any of it, using the money only for a couple of meals, a movie, and some toothpaste. I didn't think I should keep the money so when I returned to the house, where I was renting two rooms, to get my stuff I gave the money to the landlady. I flew back to Detroit with the Lions.

The rest, as they say, is history.

You can't talk about NFL history without including Baltimore and the great Unitas. The Colts won three NFL championships—one of those coming the season when I ultimately signed with the Lions—and a Super Bowl in 40 years. I was glad to see after the Colts left for Indianapolis in 1983 that the NFL returned to Baltimore in 1996. The Ravens won the Super Bowl just four years later and by 2008 had become the chief rivals of the Steelers.

Most of our games in that era were knockdown, drag-out, low-scoring games. We had beaten the Ravens 23–20 in overtime in late September, and that qualified as a veritable shootout. This time when we met, a touchdown would not be scored in the first 59 minutes of the game.

The Ravens had an interesting game plan. They were determined to run the ball and went with an unbalanced offensive line with an extra tackle an inordinate amount of times. They didn't think they could block LaMarr Woodley and James Harrison. They wanted to slow Harrison down by keeping more than one big guy on his side a lot. They had two pretty big, strong backs in Le'Ron McClain and Willis McGahee. They also had Lorenzo Neal, one of the best fullbacks who ever played and maybe the last great NFL fullback. With Ray Rice out because of an injury, they were just going to ground and pound.

We probably would have pulled them out of that earlier, but special teams played such an outsized factor in the game. We intercepted Flacco twice and held him to 11 completions on 28 attempts. We outgained the Ravens 311 to 202 yards, but they led the whole dadgum game because of field position. The Ravens' average starting field position was their 45-yard line; ours was the 22-yard line. I really admired Ravens safety Jim Leonhard. He played hard and smart, a lot like our safeties. He set the tone in this game—not as a defensive back but as a return man. He returned the opening kickoff to Baltimore's 39-yard line. Early in the second quarter, his 46-yard punt return led to the first score of the game, a short Matt Stover field goal. The first half was a punting battle. Given Leonhard's impact as a returner, we were probably lucky to only be trailing 6–3 at halftime.

The defense really hung in there in the first half. After an 18-yard Leonhard punt return—yes, that guy again—in the second quarter, Flacco threw to a hook route against a rotated defense. We did a good job of disguising our coverage, and Ike Taylor tipped the ball. Ryan Clark reacted from the deep zone and came over and made the interception. It was a hell of a catch by Clark and a great break on the ball by Taylor. That gave us the ball on our own 33-yard line and the first time we had any breathing room.

The Ravens would have had to loosen up more on offense if not for the great field position they had. The way they were running right at us wasn't successful, but they were winning, so they stayed right with it. We got the ball after halftime and went three-and-out, and Baltimore only had a 10-yard return, which was good. After they made a first down, Aaron Smith made a great move on a second-effort play and sacked Flacco for an 11-yard loss, forcing a punt. With the speed that we had and the blitzers we had, if we got a team to second and 21, it was usually very difficult for an offense to get a first down out of it.

Baltimore continued to match our defense and sacked Ben Roethlisberger on third down, getting the ball back on its own 42-yard line after the punt. Smith had another really good rush on third down that caused an incompletion and forced a punt. I think this was one of Smith's better games, and that is saying something. He was one of the most underrated defensive linemen that I've ever seen. He almost never was blocked. He was out there with Harrison and Woodley and Casey Hampton and Troy Polamalu, so you didn't hear enough about how good Smith was. He and Brett Keisel were playmakers and big guys, and both of them could run. Smith's name showed up in this game a lot.

Midway through the third quarter, special teams showed up again and, keeping with the theme of the game, not in our favor. The Ravens pinned us on the 1-yard line after a 56-yard punt. Roethlisberger hit Santonio Holmes with a 10-yard pass, but he fumbled, and Ed Reed recovered at our 16-yard line. There had been a lot of weird plays, and they had all gone against us. McClain gained six yards on two carries, and on third down, Flacco threw an incomplete pass. We held up against great adversity, and Baltimore kicked a field goal to increase its lead to 9–3.

We finally caught a break near the end of the quarter. Holmes had a punt bounce off his shoulder pads and toward where the Ravens had punted. It bounced off one of the Ravens' helmets, and our guy, Keyaron Fox, scooped up the loose ball. He returned it to the Baltimore 33. We gave the ball back after Roethlisberger was sacked and fumbled, but on our next possession, he completed a 30-yard pass to Hines Ward.

If one player was built for Steelers–Ravens, it was Ward. Of all the great receivers that I've been associated with—and there are a lot—if somebody came to me and said, "LeBeau, you've got one guy that we're sending over the middle to catch the ball, and he's got to catch the ball for your life," I'm taking Ward because he's going to come back with that football. He was an amazing guy in the fact that nothing bothered him. Nothing was ever too tough for him, and the tougher it got, the better he played. There's no question in my mind that he's a Pro Football Hall of Famer.

His catch led to a Jeff Reed field goal that got us to within three points with six minutes left to play. Baltimore came close to putting the game away on the next drive. Flacco hit passes of 19 and 11 yards, and McClain had a 10-yard run. On third and 8 from our 27-yard line, Lawrence Timmons made a great play. He sacked Flacco and forced a fumble, but Baltimore recovered it at the 41-yard line.

Timmons really came into his own in his second season, and we were fortunate to have such quality depth on that team. Even though we had taken him with the 15th overall pick of the 2007 NFL Draft, we had the luxury of bringing him along and not rushing him into action. Timmons developed skill and knowledge in two different areas: inside and outside linebacker. That just magnified his importance to the team later on in his career. He checked all the boxes we look for as far as size, speed, and competitiveness. His sack of Flacco displayed that.

It also showed what made this group so special. Timmons came free on a fire-zone blitz, and it was as much as what the others players did, too, that allowed him to get the sack. A lot of times, sacks come off an orchestrated blitz. The guys who can seal, maneuver, and confuse the blockers are often just as critical as the guy getting in there making the sack. I never cared too much who got the sack and I preached that to a great extent. The sack is a result of team execution. There's got to be enough coverage that the quarterback can't throw the ball somewhere right away. If blitzers don't have a little bit of time, they're unable to get there. That was always our concept: a sack was a team sack, and we always looked where we ranked in sacks as a team.

Baltimore opted to punt after Timmons' sack, and Holmes made a fair catch on our 8-yard line. After not scoring a touchdown all game, we had to drive the length of the field in a hostile stadium against a really good defense in under four minutes. Roethlisberger and Ward connected on 13-yard passes to start the drive. On third and 10 from our 34-yard line, he completed a 16-yard pass to Nate Washington for a critical first down. Roethlisberger was terrific on this drive, and these situations always seemed to bring out the best in him. He completed 7-of-10 passes for 89 yards when Baltimore knew we had to throw the ball. His last completion came after one of his patented scrambles on third down. He found Holmes just inside goal line, and Holmes held onto the pass after taking a shot. It was one of those bang-bang plays that made it hard to tell if Holmes had caught the ball just beyond the goal line. After a long review, the ruling on the field of a touchdown was upheld.

Reed made the extra point, which was critical because it gave us a four-point lead with 50 seconds left in the game. On the point after, our holder, Mitch Berger, and a Baltimore rusher got a little chippy. Reed came over and didn't do much. He put his hands on the guy, and they called a 15-yard unsportsmanlike conduct penalty. We had to kick off from the 15-yard line, and Baltimore got the ball to our 40 yard line. They were close enough for a Hail Mary, my least favorite play in football. Flacco cut it loose, but Will Gay played the ball great and picked it off to seal the game. Not that I had any questions about it, but this game showed our mettle as much as any in the regular season. We had led for all of 50 seconds—yet left Baltimore with a win that all but clinched a second straight AFC North title. The regular season had produced two classic Steelers–Ravens games, and we would see them again very shortly.

One of Patton's Favorite Soldiers

Dick LeBeau's 14-year playing career with the Detroit Lions led him to the Pro Football Hall of Fame. At the start of it though, he had trouble getting into his own locker room. A fifth-round draft pick of the Cleveland Browns in 1959, LeBeau was one of the final players cut. The Ohio State cornerback signed with the Lions' taxi squad after spending a few days on the Baltimore Colts' taxi squad.

About a month into the season, the Lions promoted LeBeau to their active roster. That is when things got interesting. "The first game I played was a home game and I went over to Briggs Stadium. I go up to the players' entrance, and the guard stops me," LeBeau said. "He said, 'You're not a player. I know all the players.' I can't get in the stadium, and an equipment man was walking by, and I yelled to him, 'This guy won't let me in.' He told the guard I was a player, and that was my debut for the Detroit Lions. I almost didn't get in, but I made 172 straight games after that."

Indeed, LeBeau became a fixture in the Lions' secondary, one of the best of its era, and a fan favorite. After a career in which he intercepted 62 passes, LeBeau received a memorable reminder of how far he came from that humbling start to his Lions career. A defensive backs coach for the Green Bay Packers, LeBeau was playing in the Vince Lombardi Charity Golf Tournament in Milwaukee. It attracted NFL coaches and celebrities of all kinds, including actor George C. Scott, the year LeBeau played in the event.

At a dinner that concluded the event, LeBeau and his wife, Nancy, were at a table with almost 20 other people, and they were talking about Scott, who had won an Academy Award for his portrayal of U.S. general George S. Patton in the eponymous movie *Patton.* "We were about 70 yards from his table, so it didn't look like we were going to get close to him," LeBeau recalled. "Scott gets up there to speak and thanks everyone and says, 'I want to announce right now that there is one guy I want to meet before I leave here and I don't know where you are out there, but I want to meet Dick LeBeau.' Everybody is looking at me."

After the event a member of Scott's party approached LeBeau and asked if he and Nancy would have a drink with Scott and his wife. They eagerly accepted, and while chatting with Scott, LeBeau learned that he was from Detroit and a huge Lions fan. Scott said that he had met almost all of LeBeau's former teammates and did not want to miss out on the opportunity to meet LeBeau. "That was like a one in a million deal," LeBeau said.

—G.V.B.

15

Singing the Holiday Blues

I come from a musical family. My dad was a drummer in a band and always had music on in the house. My brother, Bob, can get music out of anything. He plays about four different instruments and is a big-band jazz guy. He's played in two or three bands a week all of his life. He's 89 and he still plays. When they play they get good crowds. I like to play the guitar and I always sang in high school and choirs in church.

Given my background and love of music, I guess it is fitting that I played my entire career in Detroit. The whole music industry revolved around Detroit then, and we knew all the Motown guys. After home games the whole team ate together. We celebrated if we won. We commiserated if we lost. Teams don't do that anymore, but 90 percent of the team would go to dinner at the bottom of a Detroit restaurant. The owners isolated that room just for us and any family guests. A lot of times Motown guys would be down there, and we would sing. Football and Motown intersected quite often when I was in Detroit.

Lem Barney and Mel Farr and a couple other players from the Lions were the background singers for Marvin Gaye on his *What's Going On* album. Gaye came over and played football with us one Saturday before a game. It was a relaxed game, mostly touch. He was not NFL quality—let's put it that way—but, boy, could he sing.

Barney was also good friends with Diana Ross. After she became a big star, she moved to Los Angeles, and Barney stopped by her house one day while he was out there. It was this huge mansion, and the maid answered the door. He told her who he was and that he was a real good friend of Ross. She told him to have a seat, and there was a waiting room. She returned seven or eight minutes later and said, "Diana says she's too busy today. She can't see you." Barney started throwing a fit. He always talked about this and how she wouldn't even see him when he went over that day. You better believe we had some fun with Barney about that.

We experienced a more somber moment as teammates in 1963 after a promoter had gotten a license to record Lions-themed Christmas carols on 78 LP records that were later sold at home games. They put together a little choral group and had about 10 of us singing Christmas carols. We were recording when a guy came into the studio and said John F. Kennedy had just been shot. The nation was in shock and mourning after his assassination, and there was a great deal of discussion of whether the NFL was going to play the games that Sunday. As a professional athlete, you just waited for the powers that be to make a decision. My feeling was I signed a contract, and my contract was to play games if they played them. You talked to your children and your fellow citizens about commitments and contracts, and your word is the strongest asset you have, and it was not an easy decision, I'm sure, for many. Everybody was so sad, but I don't remember anyone saying they didn't want to play.

Just as fitting as my NFL career starting in Detroit was it ending in Nashville, the epicenter of country music. I left the Pittsburgh Steelers after the 2014 season and spent three seasons with the Tennessee Titans as an assistant head coach and defensive coordinator. I really enjoyed my time there, though I did not have much time to experience the music scene because I was so busy with football. I did go to a place called Brown's Diner a couple of times before I left Nashville. Musicians hang around there, and I played guitar a couple of times at Brown's after I got to know the guys who ran the place. There are a million great artists in Nashville.

It is also where I had one of the most enjoyable and memorable experiences of my life, one that was over a decade in the making. Garth Brooks has always been a big Steelers fan and he had been a pretty accomplished athlete before becoming a country music megastar. During one of his first big tours of the country, he played Pittsburgh and asked if he could come to the facility. That was the first time I ever met him. I just got to shake his hand and say hello. Some of the guys, Brett Keisel in particular, were big fans of country music and became friends with him. Brooks, as it turned out, was a huge fan of our defense.

While I was coaching for the Titans, I got a call one day from Michele Rosenthal. We had worked together in Pittsburgh when she was the Steelers' community relations director. She later became Keisel's assistant after he started a really successful business talking to CEOs, presidents, and other leaders about team building and teamwork. I had played a song or two with Keisel, and Rosenthal had heard me play guitar one night. I did not expect to ever get a call from her saying that Brooks wanted to meet me and asking if I would go to his house. I said, "Are you kidding me?"

The funniest part about it is I just walked in there carrying my guitar case, and we sat down and exchanged a few pleasantries. I opened up my guitar case and started playing and singing for about an hour—for Garth Brooks for God's sake! I had learned six or seven of his songs and I sang them all. He was impressed that I could remember the lyrics to all of his songs. I said, "Well, Garth, we've got 50 blitzes, and I've got 11 different positions that I've got to know what they do on 50 different blitzes. Your songs are pretty easy."

We didn't talk football that much. Most of the time we were playing and singing. I still can't believe it. He's sold more records than anybody, and I was playing, and he was sitting on his couch with his wife, Trisha Yearwood, listening. Boy, that had to be painful for them, but he acted like he was doing okay with it. The thing that surprised me is that maybe at first I was a little nervous but not really after that. I enjoy playing the guitar. I know I'm a pretty damn good defensive coordinator and I also know I'm not much of a guitar player and singer. I just like to do it and I did it.

One enduring memory from that visit happened when we were having some sandwiches while waiting for Yearwood to finish shooting her TV show. My wife, Nancy; our son, Brandon; and his wife, Bonnie, were with us. Keisel and Rosenthal were the other guests. Brandon and Bonnie had just had a son, and Bennett was only a couple of months old. He was fussing a little bit when we sat down for some sandwiches. Brooks walked over and picked him up out of his highchair. They've got a pretty nice house, and Brooks walked Bennett around the kitchen, which was probably about a 40-yard lap, for about a half an hour. We've got pictures of it. It was just a super night—not quite like winning the Super Bowl but right next to it.

I wish my memories from the Steelers' trip to Nashville on December 21, 2008, were anywhere close to that night at Brooks' house. Alas, that is where our five-game winning streak came to a screeching halt. I don't think any of us expected the game to play out the way it did—at least in the second half. We had everything to play for even after clinching the AFC North title with that last-second win in Baltimore. We were 11–3, and the Titans were 12–2, and if we won at Tennessee for the first time since 2001, we would get an early Christmas present: home-field advantage throughout the AFC playoffs, assuming we didn't stub our toe the following week against the Cleveland Browns.

We fell behind 10–0 in the first half, and a couple of plays showed that maybe it was not going to be our day. Late in the first quarter, Ben Roethlisberger looked like he was going to score a touchdown, but he got hit and fumbled. Tennessee recovered the loose ball at the 1-yard line, and our defense could not keep the Titans hemmed in there. Two runs gave them a first down and some breathing room. Kerry Collins threw a 26-yard pass to Justin Gage, and Tennessee completely flipped the field when punter Craig Hentrich pinned us at our own 3-yard line. That swing led to a Titans field goal.

Another lost fumble by Roethlisberger set up the first touchdown of the game, but he quickly stabilized us. He and Willie Parker keyed a 10-play, 80-yard drive that Roethlisberger capped with a 31-yard touchdown pass to Santonio Holmes. We went into halftime trailing 10–7 and finally took the lead in the third quarter. Roethlisberger went to work with Holmes and Hines Ward, who made a great catch down the middle at the 8-yard line and then eluded two defenders for the 21-yard touchdown.

We did not get to enjoy the lead for long. Collins hit some quick passes on Tennessee's ensuing possession. On third and 8 from Tennessee's 37-yard line, we needed a stop to get off the field, but Collins hooked up with Gage again—this time on 21-yard pass play. Collins killed us on this drive. We sacked him once as James Harrison dropped him for a 10-yard loss to set a Steelers single-season record with his 16th sack. But two plays later on third and Chattanooga, Collins completed a 19-yard pass to Justin McCareins to our 21-yard line. Tennessee went for it on fourth and 1, and I threw the kitchen sink at them. Chris Johnson got the ball on a toss sweep, and the one guy, who had a chance at tackling the speedster, slipped on the slick field, and Johnson was gone.

The game really started to tilt on the next possession when Michael Griffin intercepted a deep Roethlisberger pass and returned it all the way to our 37-yard line. We were still only down 17–14, but we couldn't get off the field—or stay out of our own way. We got the Titans to fourth and 1 from our 4-yard line, and they elected to take the easy field goal. We were called for unsportsmanlike conduct during the kick, and that gave them a first down on our 2-yard line. On the first play of the fourth quarter, LenDale White barreled into the end zone from the 1-yard line to give the Titans a 24–14 lead, and Tennessee controlled the game the rest of the way.

Griffin returned an interception 83 yards in the waning moments of the game to punctuate Tennessee's 31–14 win. The game was much closer than the final score indicated, and we beat ourselves as much as the Titans did. We had four turnovers and did not have a takeaway. You're not going to win many games having to overcome that, and we were playing a Super Bowl contender on its home field. It was just a bad day all around.

We only sacked Collins one time and gave up 322 yards of total offense. It was the first time we had given up more than 300 yards that season. Also uncharacteristic of our defense was our inability to make a play to get off the field. I was always a positive person after a game and I made it a point to go to all of our players on offense and defense. They were great competitors, and I knew that we had an excellent chance to beat anybody any time we went out there. That was my message, and I thought we would be back in Nashville real soon for a rematch.

A Yuletide Tradition

One of the great traditions that Dick LeBeau had during his time with the Pittsburgh Steelers was reciting "The Night Before Christmas" for the team during the holiday season. "I did it pretty much from the first or second year with Coach Cowher," said LeBeau, who came to the Steelers as a defensive backs coach in Cowher's first year in 1992.

LeBeau performed the iconic poem in Cincinnati, where he coached before coming to Pittsburgh. But a tradition that was so unique in the cutthroat NFL for so many reasons—imagine Bill Belichick...well, never mind—is rooted in LeBeau's upbringing. He grew up in London, Ohio, and came of age during World War II when rationing was the norm, and every penny counted. "My family was mostly women, and they were lovers of Christmas," LeBeau recalled. "The women worked all year to make Christmas special. You would have thought we were the Rockefellers when Christmas came. As a little kid, you can't believe the impact that had on your family and what they sacrificed to provide for their family. I said, 'What can I do to show these women that the spirit of Christmas lives in me?'"

They probably never imagined he would take it to the length he did. "I learned 'The Night Before Christmas,' and that was before I knew how many verses there were. It's longer than you think," LeBeau said. "But I started doing it for my family and I wanted to do it for my extended family: my players."

His performances extended to the entire team at the request of Cowher, and it took on a life of its own. "It's a magnetic poem, and we raised money for charity and the hospitals around Pittsburgh," LeBeau said. "There's enough ham in me that I had no problem going through all the hand gestures I loved to share. The poem always was well received by any audience of any size. I did it everywhere, but it was bigger in Pittsburgh than any place."

The players loved LeBeau reciting the poem. "You would think guys who had been here six, seven years would get tired of it," longtime defensive line and assistant coach John Mitchell said. "But when December came, every day they would come in and tease Dick, 'Hey, get your act together. We're looking forward to 'The Night Before Christmas.'"

NFL players mesmerized by LeBeau reciting a Christmas poem made for an interesting juxtaposition given their profession. "It's crazy. You've got the alphas of the alphas and you're in a meeting with a bunch of alpha males that play professional football, which is a violent game," defensive end Aaron Smith said. "The mindset is there, and you get this guy, who stands up there and starts this poem the night before a game, but he's so animated and so into it. You feel like you're a kid in kindergarten watching some guy perform a scene in front of you and you're just captivated by it."

Ike Taylor compared it to kids waiting to sit on Santa Claus' lap, another time-honored tradition that takes most back to their youth. "We couldn't wait until Coach LeBeau stood before everybody and recited that poem," he said. "We are talking about grown men between the age of 23 and 60. It's crazy."

During the pandemic, when people were forced to celebrate Christmas in groups that rarely exceeded family, LeBeau and the players gathered on a Zoom call. LeBeau performed his famous rendition of "The Night Before Christmas" for them and their loved ones. "My family couldn't believe that we got to see that every single year," nose tackle Casey Hampton said. "That is crazy, and we still talk about that to this day."

After LeBeau was finished, no one wanted to get off the call. "We were on the Zoom probably six, seven hours that night," linebacker Larry Foote said. "Eventually his wife kicked him off."

—G.V.B.

16

Hollywood (Regular-Season) Ending

As many stars and great players as we had in 2008, you cannot write the story of that team without talking about the overall strength of our roster. We had incredible depth, especially on defense. Players like Chris Hoke, Travis Kirschke, Nick Eason, Tyrone Carter, and William Gay were among those who helped us weather injuries, which were a recurring theme that season. Brett Keisel and Casey Hampton missed nine games between them because of injuries. Cornerbacks Deshea Townsend and Bryant McFadden missed 11 games between them. Free safety Ryan Clark could not play in two games because of injuries.

It helped that our top five linebackers only missed two games among them, but I was surprised at how many different players we had to use so quickly on both sides of the ball. Our defense never suffered, and that started up front. Nobody could run the ball on us, and in the four games that Hoke started for Hampton, we did not miss a beat statistically.

Hokie really embodied that next-man-up mentality, and with this team, it was not just a mantra. He was a great competitor, and great competitors don't want to get their picture in front of the whole team during film review for suffering a defensive breakdown. Hoke was going to make sure his picture was up there holding up his end of the deal. He had excellent quickness and a tremendous center of gravity, which is critical for nose tackles. Hoke was blessed with a real fast-thinking mind and he could counter situations that maybe some NFL guys couldn't get out of. He would get out of them because he would see an opening and be quick to exploit it. He was just a really, really good football player and probably would have started in 90 percent of the NFL lineups. He just happened to be behind Hampton.

What proved beneficial—and part of it was philosophical—was we rotated our defensive line. That is why players like Hoke, Kirschke, and Eason were so critical to our success. To execute and perform at the level that we wanted to for 60 minutes, we had to get all of them out there to share the load and not ask just three guys to play 72 snaps. We rotated our big guys quite a bit, particularly with the weather in mind, knowing that before the year was over we were going to need every one of them in that room. That was what we preached from Day One, and these guys bought into it. They all prepared as if they were going to be playing the whole game, and so when we got to the games where they had to play three-fourths of it or all of it, they were ready to go. This season only reinforced what my football career had taught me: you need a strong supporting cast because of the inevitability of injuries and the grind that is an NFL season.

My playing career had once exposed me to a different kind of supporting cast, one that eventually led to me practicing an English accent with the great actor Michael Caine in the Philippines. In the 1960s the Pro Bowl was played in Los Angeles, and it was a real game. Players didn't have all the money they've got now, and the winning team earned $3,000 or $4,000 extra. Nobody passed it up. There was a pretty large Hollywood contingent out there, and I met Robert Aldrich through the Pro Bowl. Aldrich had become a pretty big cinematic director after *What Ever Happened to Baby Jane*, a takeoff on a Hollywood murder. He was also known for directing *The Dirty Dozen*, which came out in 1967 and starred Charles Bronson and the late, great Jim Brown among others.

He was working on another war picture. This one was about a group of coast watchers in World War II, going behind the lines in the South Pacific and watching the naval channels for movement of the Japanese fleet. Twenty English guys were in *Too Late the Hero*, including Caine, and there was one American played by Cliff Robertson. One of Aldrich's good friends was Eddie Meador, who played safety for the Los Angeles Rams and was an All-Pro player. He came to me one day after a Pro Bowl practice and said, "I'd like you to come meet Robert Aldrich."

And then Meador unexpectedly said, "He wants to talk to you about a movie."

I said, "What the hell does he want to talk to me about?"

He said, "I don't know. It's something about being a stunt double."

I said, "Well, I'll talk to him, sure."

They were shooting on the Philippines Islands and were going to be over there for about six weeks. It was in the middle of the jungle where the average temperature was 105 when they were going to shoot. They were going to shoot a scene 12, 15 times, and in the scene, stuntmen would run 75 to 150 yards, but it was all zigzagging, so they were probably running 300 yards at a time, and in 25, 30 minutes, they'd run it again. The ordinary stuntman would have lasted about twice. Aldrich wanted two football players because he loved the NFL and he knew they would never be able to stay on schedule with regular stuntmen. Pat Studstill, our punter, looked a little bit like Robertson, who had just won an Academy Award. He got cast as his stunt double. I got cast as Caine's stunt double.

It was hard work, and glamourous isn't the word I would choose to describe my big-screen experience. We were on location for five weeks in the jungle and stayed in a little stucco building with some rooms in it. There was one woman in the whole damn camp. She was the business director or something like that, and there were 500 men. It was 60 minutes to the set if you went by truck, but if you cut across the bay, we could get there in about 20 minutes, so I took the boat every morning. We stayed on the set all day, and every time they shot a scene, they had to reload all of the explosive stuff, so there was an hour where we would sit down just trying to get out of the sun. No one could go anywhere. So I got to talk Caine and I got to be pretty friendly with him. One day I said to Aldrich, "Robert, damn it, I've got to have a line. You've got to get me on camera speaking. I can't just be running around across the damn rice patty fields."

He said, "How in the hell am I going to get you a line? These guys are all English. If you can do an English accent, I might get you a line."

They had a couple of tents with pool tables and shuffleboard to kill time when we were waiting for them to shoot. Caine liked to play pool, and I was a decent pool player, so we'd shoot pool a little bit. I felt like I got to know him well enough so one day I said, "Michael, Robert said he'd give me a couple of lines in this movie if I get some kind of accent. Why don't you teach me a British accent?"

He said, "We'll do Cockney. That's the easiest."

We worked on that until Caine said, "Ah yeah, Dick, you're ready to go."

A couple of days later, I went over to Aldrich's tent when he was on a break. I said, "Bob, I think I got that accent we were talking about."

He said, "Oh, LeBeau, when are you going to give up?"

I said, "Well, the boys back home, they've got to hear me have a line."

He said, "All right, let me hear it."

Using my best British accent, I said, "There's a light out by the billiard table." I thought I was pretty damn good. So I said, "What do you think of that?"

He said, 'You sound like a hillbilly trying to sound like a Cockney. Get the hell out of here."

I never would have gone over there if Caine hadn't said I had the accent. I didn't get a line, but it was a great experience.

Our 2008 team had it all—stars and a supporting cast—which made the loss in Tennessee so surprising. None of us expected to lose to the Titans by 17 points, but I wasn't worried about any sort of hangover. We didn't lose very many, but when we did, we almost always played well the next week. There's no better motivation than having a bad game. You're going to get invested in the next one.

That was a characteristic of this bunch of guys not only that year, but also throughout their careers. They were going to compete. You're playing against the best offenses in the world, and some Sundays ain't going to go the way you want them to go, but I always felt good about our chances to rebound and play well because we were consistently sound in what we were doing, and the effort was a plus. More often than not, we were going to get our share of plays made.

That certainly proved to be the case in our regular-season finale at Heinz Field. Even without James Harrison, who did not play because of a hip injury, our defense got back on track in a big way. The Cleveland Browns managed just 20 passing yards, and Bruce Gradkowski posted a quarterback rating of 1.0. Again showing the depth we had on defense, Carter picked off two of his passes. The second one he returned 32 yards for a touchdown, capping the scoring in our 31–0 win.

The victory clinched a second-straight AFC North title and gave us the No. 2 seed in the AFC playoffs. Really, the only drama from the game came late in the second quarter. Ben Roethlisberger had to be carted off the field with a head injury and did not return. As always, we were in good hands with Byron Leftwich, and his eight-yard touchdown run before halftime gave us a 14–0 lead. Even better: Roethlisberger's injury turned out to be a scare more than anything else.

The whole team had earned a well-deserved chance to recharge before the playoffs started. We had won 12 games against four losses while playing the toughest schedule in the NFL. We had overcome our share of injuries along the way, something that spoke not only to our depth, but also to the players in our locker room. There were never any problems that spilled over, and I think that was due to the great leadership on that team. They all were invested. A team is the total of its individual ingredients. They all put their talents into a box, and the best teams don't care who gets the credit. We're all filling up the box to get where we had to get to be successful. You're going to have different personalities, but the most successful championship teams have guys who are unselfish and competitive. We had both in abundance—not to mention so many special players at different positions. Would it be enough as we were about to embark on tournament play? We were about to find out.

When Hollywood Came Calling (Kind of)

Not long after the Pittsburgh Steelers picked Bryant McFadden in the second round of the 2005 NFL Draft, his mother made an observation about one of his new coaches. "Your defensive coordinator looks like Clint Eastwood," she told her son.

Dick LeBeau was not Dirty Harry, perhaps the most famous character that Eastwood has played during an illustrious acting career. But he indeed had the looks of a movie star. That is what a friend, who owned an upscale bar in Los Angeles that was a Hollywood hangout, told him while LeBeau was playing for the Detroit Lions. He offered to set up a meeting with well-known producer Sheldon Leonard, who had also acted in scores of movies, including, *It's a Wonderful Life.* LeBeau has always been guided by the belief that it never hurts to listen, so he agreed to a meeting.

Leonard made it clear that he was interested in LeBeau but wanted him to undergo training and get experience in summer theater. "I said, 'I ain't looking for no acting lessons. I'm a football player. It's nice meeting you, but I'm going to take a pass on this,'" LeBeau recalled. "That was as close as I came to acting."

LeBeau did work as a stunt man in *Too Late the Hero*, a World War II movie that was released in 1970. He also appeared on the *Super Comedy Bowl.* Broadcast the week before the Super Bowl, the nationally televised show featured Carol Burnett as the host and NFL players as the talent. LeBeau sang and played guitar on the show one year. He remembers it as much for his appearance as for how he performed. "I wore a Harry Belafonte get-up with tight-fitting, bell-bottom pants and a big, old, fluffy-ass shirt cut down to the stomach," LeBeau said, laughing. "I was Charlie Potatoes, man."

—S.B.

17

Charging Forward

During the early part of my NFL playing career, I played a round of golf at Scioto Country Club in Upper Arlington, Ohio. Jack Nicklaus had grown up there, and I had played some golf with him when we were at Ohio State. A friend and I played at Scioto and had a beer afterward in the clubhouse. When I got back home to London, which was about 25 miles away, I discovered that I had left my umbrella in the grill room. In retrospect, I'm glad that I did.

I called another friend, Bob Hoag, who belonged to Scioto and was good friends with Nicklaus. He was a real good amateur player who later regularly teamed up with Nicklaus in the Pebble Beach Pro-Am. I called Hoag and told him I wanted to come back to the club to get my umbrella. He said, "Why don't you come tomorrow because Jack Nicklaus is getting a shipment of drivers from MacGregor, and he's going to go through them and pick out his drivers that he's going to take on tour with him this year? I thought you might want to watch him go through these drivers."

I said, "You know that's a yes."

I returned to Scioto the next day to watch Nicklaus. There were about 25 drivers in the shipment he had received, and every one supposedly had the same specifications. Nicklaus loosened up and then started hitting these drivers. The equipment then was primitive compared to now with persimmon heads and balata golf balls. But here was Nicklaus launching the ball 300, 315 yards. Every shot was identical, scraping the sky before coming down.

He threw most of the drivers on one pile. On this other pile, he had three or four that he particularly liked. I don't know how he picked a driver out of all of them because they all worked the same way. Every swing, every shot he hit was identical. He had attained through repetition the ability to be functionally sound shot after shot after shot. That display stuck with me and became a part of my philosophy, especially after I went into coaching. The goal was to have that good play every single snap and hit that 300-yard drive that comes down in the middle of the fairway. The bigger the game, the more important those fundamentals were.

And the games were only going to get bigger as we embarked on what was essentially a second season. By all measures our regular season had been successful. But when you walked past five Lombardi Trophies every time you went to your office, you knew winning division titles was not the ultimate goal.

What winning the AFC North with December come-from-behind victories against the Dallas Cowboys and Baltimore Ravens had done was guarantee us one game in the playoffs and buy us some time. If we had lost to the Cowboys or Ravens—and pretty well into the fourth quarter in both games it did not look great for us—we would have been playing the first week of the AFC playoffs in the wild-card round. It turned out that the bye we got for securing the No. 2 seed behind the Tennessee Titans came at the perfect time. Ben Roethlisberger had been knocked out of the regular-season finale against the Cleveland Browns with a concussion and he was not cleared to play until early in the week after our bye.

With Roethlisberger healthy I liked where we were, even though it looked like the AFC playoffs would run through Nashville, Tennessee. We had won five games in a row prior to losing to the Titans, and I felt like that had kind of woken us up. We had led the league in almost every defensive category, and our offense was rock solid. Everything was in front of us.

In the divisional round, we were playing the San Diego Chargers. They had beaten the Indianapolis Colts 23–17 in overtime of the wild-card round, and we knew it would be a tough game. We had beaten the Chargers at Heinz Field in November in the first 11–10 final score in NFL history. That had been the start of the five-game winning streak when I felt like we really started to come together. It had also been one of three games we had won during that span after trailing in the fourth quarter.

Suffice it to say we were not going to take the Chargers lightly, especially with the zero-sum stakes attached to the game. As close as our first game against the Chargers had been, we had dominated it statistically. The disparity in penalties—we had 13 for 115 yards, and they had two for five—had been the main reason why we needed Roethlisberger to lead a drive that resulted in a Jeff Reed game-winning field goal with 11 seconds left to play.

That game was a textbook example of why that day when I watched that sublime display of Nicklaus hitting really resonated with me when it came to the playoffs. No, we did not have to be perfect, as Nicklaus seemingly was that day. But we could not have one good play followed by a bad or a so-so play. If we were consistent, we had so many unique and special players that we could beat anybody.

If one player defined consistency as a player and as a person, it was Heath Miller. He is simply one of the greatest tight ends I was ever with during my time in the NFL. If you got the ball anywhere near Miller, it was almost always getting caught. It was so rare when he did miss that you couldn't help but say, "What the hell happened there?" He was a totally unique talent who impacted our offense the way Rob Gronkowski did for the New England Patriots.

One time I was in an airport changing planes, and a guy came up to me and asked if I was Coach LeBeau. He had been an umpire in the ACC for years, and I think at that point he was an officer of the conference's officiating crews. He said, "I just wanted to ask you about Heath Miller and how he's doing."

I said, "He's doing fantastic. He's the best tight end in the NFL."

He said, "I'm glad to hear that because when he played in college of all the games that I've officiated and all the athletes I've followed where their careers are he was the most consistently polite and perfectly behaved football player that I've ever had."

I said, "I'm passing that right on to Heath," which I did.

That is a perfect description of the way he is. He was amazingly consistent. I just don't recall him ever not getting his part of it done. Sure enough, he came through against the Chargers catching a touchdown pass in our 35–24 win at Heinz Field. Miller's score came in the third quarter when we took control of what had been a close game.

San Diego struck first, needing only four plays to go 75 yards for a touchdown on the first possession of the game. Vincent Jackson get behind us on a play-action pass and he caught a beautiful 41-yard touchdown pass from Philip Rivers. I'm guessing that made a few of our fans uneasy because of what had happened the last time San Diego visited Pittsburgh in the postseason. That had been in the 1994 AFC Championship Game when we had an outstanding chance to go to the Super Bowl. We led the Chargers 13–3 in the second half, but they threw a pair of 43-yard touchdown passes, including one with about five minutes left to play, and they upset us 17–13 at Three Rivers Stadium.

I did not have flashbacks to that day nor was I particularly worried after Rivers' early touchdown pass to Jackson. It had been a perfectly thrown pass, and sometimes you have to tip your cap to the other guys, who are also professionals. Being a defensive coordinator, a defensive backs coach, and a defensive back all of my life, I know that can happen anytime with the amazing and skilled athletes on the offensive side of the ball. If they throw it just right and you're up against a top athlete, they're going to make a big play on it, and that's what happened.

Midway through the first quarter, we answered with a big play of our own to even the score. After driving to the Chargers' 34-yard line, we lined up to go for it on fourth down. Just before the snap, Roethlisberger dropped back to a punting position and he pooched one that went out of bounds at the 9-yard line. We held San Diego to three-and-out, and

Santonio Holmes returned the punt 67 yards for a touchdown. It was a huge play. The Chargers had beaten the Colts the previous week primarily because they kept flipping the field with Mike Scifres, who averaged almost 53 yards per punt.

Winning a special teams battle in that fashion gave us a lift when we needed it. So did a touchdown drive at the end of the first half. We were trailing 10–7 when Roethlisberger completed a 41-yard pass to Hines Ward. Willie Parker followed that with a three-yard scoring run, giving us a 14–10 lead at halftime.

We doubled-dipped in the third quarter with a long touchdown drive that set the tone for the rest of the game. Parker's running and Roethlisberger's passing culminated in an eight-yard touchdown catch by Miller. The game turned in the third quarter because we could run the ball, and San Diego couldn't. LaDainian Tomlinson did not play because of a groin injury, but we hardly got a bargain in facing Darren Sproles. Small but shifty, he was a big play waiting to happen. He took a flare pass 62 yards for a touchdown after we got a little sloppy. But that came late in the fourth quarter after we had put the game away and made the final score cosmetically close.

We had been a third-quarter team during the regular season, and this game might have been our best of those quarters yet. We controlled the ball to such an extent that Chargers ran just one play. On that play Larry Foote made a fantastic interception, diving to secure the catch after the ball had gotten tipped at the line of scrimmage. He and James Harrison were in such good position that each made a play on the ball. Either could have come up with the interception.

One of the things about our defense during that period—particularly that season—was they were amazingly conditioned and wonderfully coordinated athletes. Each one of them was capable of making that type of play. They were tremendously skilled athletes for the positions they were playing at every spot on the defense. Part of their total success was the fact that there wasn't anybody offenses could isolate and say, "We're going to have continued success." Everybody has good and bad plays, but at the end of the day, you weren't going to find a weak link in that defense.

Foote's pick led to the touchdown that put us up 28–10 and for all intents and purposes punched our ticket to the AFC Championship Game. Foote was such an unsung player on our defense, and he and James Farrior played so well together. I never viewed them as any different position-wise because they were interchangeable as the buck and the mack. By definition the buck, which Farrior played, is a strongside inside linebacker, and the mack is the weakside inside linebacker.

But defense is all stimulus and response. You're always reacting to the offense, and the offense is always initiating the play and the snap count on the run or the pass. The minute the offense motions the tight end across the formation, what started as the closed side ended up the open side and vice versa. Foote became the buck as soon as that tight end motioned across the formation, and Farrior became the mack. The run gap and the hole responsibility and the flow responsibility for each essentially did not change. They had to do the same things and just know whether they're on the closed side or the open side of the formation that the offense is in at the snap. That was always the first day teaching lesson for me when I was putting in the defense: where are you when the ball is snapped?

That answers every single what-if question that a player can come up with. Tell me what formation the offense was in when the ball was snapped. I don't care how many times the players shifted or how many times they motioned. When the opposition had the ball, they were in the formation that told you what you do. Ryan Clark and Troy Polamalu had to be strongside and weakside safeties of what side they were on. You can't be running around, flipping around all day long. You wouldn't get anything done.

Having interchangeable players in the middle of our defense was critical to our success that season, and all those guys were like having a coach on the field. Foote had no background in law, but I always said if I ever had to go to court and was involved in a lawsuit against me, he was going to be my lawyer because he never, ever lost a verbal argument. He was a chatterbox and he was famous among his teammates for causing all kinds of ruckus out on the field because he would very rarely just be quiet and play football. He always had something to say. And I was sure he would have plenty to say in the AFC Championship Game when we played an opponent we knew almost as well as ourselves.

A Players' Coach

Dick LeBeau commanded respect from his players despite rarely raising his voice while coaching them. His résumé helped. He played 14 seasons in the NFL, all with the Detroit Lions. His 62 interceptions were the fourth most in NFL history when he retired after the 1972 season. By the time he returned to the Pittsburgh Steelers as defensive coordinator in 2004—he had coached the defensive backs and coordinated the defense during his first stint with the team from 1992 to 1996—his reputation as a coach was also renowned.

Yet what endeared him to his players in many ways had nothing to do with what he had accomplished in football and everything to do with LeBeau as a person. "Coach LeBeau was the same to everyone and he was the same every day," said safety Ryan Clark, who signed with the Steelers as a free agent in 2006. "You never had to worry about walking past him and him not saying hello and asking how you were doing and him not being pleasant, which is very simple and you would hope everybody in the world would be that way. I've heard about guys being on teams and walking past coaches with their heads down, not being able to talk to them in the hallways."

LeBeau could not help but be the opposite of that. He has a folksy, self-deprecating nature, one that did not belie his reputation as much as it confirmed that he never strayed from his small-town roots and what his parents instilled in him about treating others. What made his players love him—and to never want to let him down—was that he treated them as people first. "When I first came [to the Steelers], if you made a mistake the day before and the coach saw you, that was the first thing the coach said to you, like, 'You've got to get down and stay in the stance. Take on that double team.' You could be eating breakfast. You could be at your locker. It didn't matter," defensive end Aaron Smith said. "They would find you, and that was the first thing they would say. I'm not saying they're wrong. I'm just saying that's the environment and the way guys are. With Coach it didn't matter. You could play horrible in a game on Sunday and come in on Monday, and he'd say, 'Good morning, 91. It's a great day to be alive!' Then he'd say, 'How's your family? How's that beautiful bride of yours.' He'd ask and talk and smile, and we'd talk about life. When you went into the meeting, that's when he would correct you, but it never was in a putting down way. He had that human side of him where he saw you as a person, not just a player. He had that relationship and he built that with you. He connected with you on that relationship level before he connected with you on the player level."

What may have resonated as much with his players as anything was his approach to others. He was the same way with a generational talent like Troy Polamalu as he was with players on the practice squad. And there was nothing contrived about it. "It didn't matter if it was someone straight off the street or the president of a company. He seemed to treat anyone with the same type of respect," defensive end Brett Keisel said. "I think that's what everyone loved about him so much: his demeanor and his attitude and the way he approached life with how he kind of held everybody in the same light and treated them with respect and class."

LeBeau's players loved their coach so much that they wore his Lions No. 44 jersey a handful of times as a tribute to him. Before a preseason game in 2007 in Canton, Ohio, the defensive players wanted to bring attention to LeBeau's playing career to the Pro Football Hall of Fame voters. They got off the bus wearing replica Lions No. 44 jerseys. LeBeau still has a picture of the players wearing his jersey hanging in the den of his suburban Cincinnati house. "That was my defense. They kept my name in the public eye in that regard, and it was very generous of them," LeBeau said. "Those are memories you take with you all your life."

The tradition got taken to another level in 2005 when the Steelers hosted the Lions in the regular-season finale. "The entire team picked No. 44 when we played Detroit, the kickers, everybody, volunteered," linebacker Larry Foote said. "We didn't ask. We weren't going around, 'Hey, we want to wear this.' That week that we played them, there were 53 jerseys hanging around the locker room, 53 jerseys hung up and probably more than that because of the practice squad guys. Everybody wanted his jersey."

When LeBeau walked into the Steelers' locker room before that game, he was stunned to see his replica jersey hanging outside of every player's locker. The jerseys—replica white Lions ones—were hanging outside of every player's locker room and from the back, so that LeBeau could see his name as he walked into the locker room. "It just went around the room in a perfect square. It was an awesome sight," LeBeau said. "I almost fell over. I got all the guys together and said, 'Look we better win this game.'"

They did win 35–21 to clinch a playoff berth and continue a run that did not end until they won the Super Bowl against the Seattle Seahawks in Detroit. As much as such gestures touched LeBeau, they were just as special for his players. "The honor was all ours, to honor him for so much that he had given us," cornerback Deshea Townsend said. "That was pride for us to wear it for him."

Nose tackle Chris Hoke still has a LeBeau replica jersey, which he wore and later had his coach sign, hanging in this closet. "We loved him so much like a father," Hoke said. "He's a special man, and you would be hard pressed to find anyone to say one bad thing about Coach LeBeau."

—G.V.B.

18

The Legend of Troy

My second coaching job in the NFL came after I had spent three seasons in Philadelphia coaching the Eagles' special teams. I went to work for the Green Bay Packers and Bart Starr, the legendary quarterback who became the franchise's head coach in 1975. Starr hired me to coach Green Bay's defensive backs in 1976, and it was an election year for president Gerald Ford. He had been an All-American center at the University of Michigan and later had a chance to play for the Packers. He opted for law school, which I think was a pretty good choice but maintained an interest in football. He had Starr participate in several of his workshops in the White House. He was on a campaign tour and he wanted to visit the facility at Green Bay. Of course, Starr said, "Sure, we'd love to have you. If it's okay, Mr. President, I'd like to have our employees meet you in the cafeteria."

President Ford came into the cafeteria, and we were all lined up, about 35 of us. He started down the line and he was not spending too much time beyond shaking hands with each person, saying, "Nice to meet you."

When he got to me, Starr said, "Mr. President, this is Dick LeBeau. You know him from your Michigan days when he played for the Detroit Lions." Well, I always thought I was a pretty cool, calm, and collected dude. I had met some famous people, movie stars, and people like that. It never did knock me off my feet. There was something different about shaking hands with the president of the United States.

He said, "Dick LeBeau, I'm a huge Detroit Lions fan. I'm so pleased to get to meet you." He's shaking my hand. Meanwhile, I'm shaking his hand like it's an old farm pump, and you're trying to get the water from the wells. I'm like an oaf making these sounds and I couldn't say anything. He said, "You're much smaller than I thought you were from watching you play."

I finally got something out and said, "Well, Mr. President, that's what everybody says when they see me."

He said, "It was a treat to get to meet you, Dick. I admired the way you played." I'll never forget that. Here was the president of the United States, and he's complimenting me. I was pretty dumbfounded by it.

With the most important game of our season on the horizon, we couldn't afford to get tongue-tied or caught up in the moment like I did with President Ford. We were playing the Baltimore Ravens for the third time in 2008, and this one was for the AFC championship.

I can honestly say that I never worried about whether our guys were going to be playing with everything they had. If you want to create stuff to worry about, there's plenty there, but in terms of confidence and trust, I never wavered with that bunch all the years that we were together. There's a trust that evolves. That had started years earlier with our defensive captain James Farrior, who was as stabilizing a force as anyone can be in professional football. He never varied. He was always focused on getting it done. He always was good for a few laughs in the locker room, but when he stepped on the practice field, it was time to go to work. The whole Pittsburgh Steelers defense was like that. I never, ever worried about them being ready for a game.

We got an unexpected bonus for the AFC Championship Game: we were playing it at home. The Ravens had upset the top-seeded Tennessee Titans in the divisional round of the AFC playoffs, setting the stage for Ravens–Steelers III at Heinz Field. We knew it would be another rock 'em, sock 'em game with the Ravens, and beating them for a third time in one season would be difficult.

They had led us for most of the game when we had played in Baltimore before Ben Roethlisberger led a 12-play, 92-yard drive at the end of the game. That produced the only touchdown of the night and a 13–9 Steelers win. We had limited rookie quarterback Joe Flacco to 11 completions on 28 attempts for 115 yards. We had also intercepted him twice and sacked him twice. Since we had already played the Ravens twice, if we had hurt them with a certain blitz, I knew damn well they were going to be ready to defend that, so they weren't going to see that.

I had a big chart on the wall in my office that whole season and I had every pressure that I had called, so I didn't have to go back and look through every film. I could just look on my board and see every blitz that we had run. If you were playing against us, you were probably not going to see the same blitzes that you saw the five games before you had last played us. The good thing about zone blitzes is you could mix and match. By that I mean you could have different patterns of the rush and coverage and yet still attack the same areas of the offense.

We were going to change constantly, and the magic of the zone blitz is that you could do that without confusing your own people. You had the platform built and you could just change this and change that. By the time you had three days of practice, it was old hat for our players but brand new for the opponents. We always did that and tried not to show them the same things that they were getting ready for against us.

Probably my biggest concern going into the game was Troy Polamalu. He could hardly practice that week because of a pulled calf muscle. We did not know going into Sunday if he would be able to play. We were making provisions for him not to play, knowing there was always a chance that he would play because he was Troy Polamalu.

Once he got loose in pregame warm-ups, he looked pretty good. He did not just play; he played a fantastic game.

We started off in great shape, stopping everything they did and moving the ball. We jumped ahead 6–0 in the first quarter on two Jeff Reed field goals. Both teams scored touchdowns in the second quarter. It was 13–7 at the half, and in the third quarter, we were controlling the ball again. Another Reed field goal produced the only points of the third quarter, and we took a nine-point lead into the fourth quarter. That is when the game got tense. We struggled to move the ball, and Baltimore got to within 16–14 after a Willis McGahee one-yard touchdown run with nine-and-a-half minutes left in the game.

We went three-and-out and caught a break when Baltimore got called for an unnecessary roughness penalty on the punt return. That backed the Ravens up to their own 14-yard-line, but they completed a 20-yard pass on the second play of the drive to keep the pressure on us. After a two-yard run, the Ravens called a timeout, and I had a chance to talk to the guys. "This is the drive," I told them. "We've got to get off the field here." Todd Heap had been a very impactful presence on the previous drive, and the Ravens hit their star tight end on every crucial down. I said to Polamalu, "I'm going to put you on Heap. Don't take your eyes off him because I'm pretty sure the ball's going to go to him. That's what I want you guys to be ready for. Get us off the field."

We went out, and Heap lined up in the backfield with McGahee, and they kept Heap in to block. They were sure that we were going to blitz, and when Polamalu saw Heap staying in and blocking, his attention went to Flacco, who turned the ball loose on a crossing pattern to Derrick Mason. He was coming open, but with Heap staying in the backfield, Polamalu intercepted that damn ball and ran it back 40 yards for a touchdown. Polamalu did what he was coached to do, and it was a little serendipitous for us. His guy was working in the backfield, and he just looked for work. He had the perfect break on the ball, and that's just Polamalu. He did that a lot of times but few in more critical situations.

If the Ravens get a field goal there, they're probably going to win the game. They had just finished driving about 80 yards for a touchdown. From being in a perilous spot, we went to easy street because Polamalu picked that damn thing off. I don't know too many people that could have made that interception, but he made it easily and he could have run 200 yards with the way he was running. He was weaving and bobbing, and they could hardly touch him. You would have never known he was injured.

There was no scoring the rest of the way, and Ryan Clark punctuated our 23–14 win with a ferocious hit on McGahee after an attempted catch that left both players prone on the Heinz Field grass. The collision proved to be a fitting metaphor for the day—and Ravens–Steelers games in general. Both teams always left everything on the field.

Roethlisberger threw for 255 yards and a touchdown. That included a 65-yard scoring pass to Santonio Holmes that gave us a 13–0 lead early in the second quarter. The defense came through when we needed it most. Polamalu's interception return for a touchdown was emblematic of that, but we played great for most of the game. We held the Ravens to 198 total yards of offense, and Flacco passed for just 141 yards while throwing three interceptions. LaMarr Woodley recorded two of our three sacks, continuing his postseason tear.

Dating back to the previous season, it was Woodley's third straight playoff game with at least two sacks. The funny thing is that after I returned to Pittsburgh in 2004, I always used to joke with Larry Foote. As an Ohio Stater, I would tell him in group settings, so we could have a laugh, "Larry, you're the only guy from Michigan that I ever loved." Then when Woodley joined the team in 2007, I'd say the same thing and add, "But, LaMarr, a couple of more sacks and you're going to get in that group."

Well, he was certainly part of that group, and his ascension that season surprised no one. He was tall, but he had a very thick frame, and his upper body strength was pretty amazing. He was almost physically perfect for an outside linebacker in a 3-4 defense. That season he probably had as many impactful plays as anybody on our defense.

He and James Harrison were a huge part of the success of that defensive group because you couldn't do anything with either one of them. You couldn't knock them off the ball to run at them and you couldn't get outside them to run around them. You had to try to find something up the middle, and there you had Casey Hampton, Farrior, and Foote.

Where were you going to go? Anybody that had a plan to try to control the game by running was just running up against a stone wall. Our 3-4 outside linebackers were the bookends, and everyone else inside could play. They were perfect for what we did. That was the perfect makeup of a 3-4 defensive team.

One of my favorite pictures from all my years in football was taken after the game. We were on the field for the presentation of the Lamar Hunt Trophy given to the AFC champion. Aaron Smith and I found each other and embraced. It had been an exhausting year for Smith, particularly after his young son, Elijah, had been diagnosed with leukemia in late October. He said, "Coach, I just want to go home and see my family." We walked off the field that day with our arms around each other. It was a special moment between a coach and player. And I can remember it like it was yesterday.

A Legacy of Linebackers

LaMarr Woodley knew he was squarely on the Pittsburgh Steelers' radar after the team hosted the University of Michigan pass rusher for a visit ahead of the 2007 NFL Draft. But when the Steelers drafted Florida State linebacker Lawrence Timmons in the first round, Woodley figured he had no chance of ending up in Pittsburgh. He, though, was still available in the second round, and the Steelers took him.

The Steelers were not the only ones elated with the pick. Woodley, a Saginaw, Michigan, native, had fallen in love with the Steelers in middle school when he moved to fullback on his football team. He immediately took jersey No. 36 and started calling himself "The Bus" after Steelers running back and Detroit native Jerome Bettis.

Whenever Woodley played *Madden NFL*, the popular video game, he always selected the Steelers and he rejoiced when they won Super Bowl XL in Detroit while he was starring at Michigan. All of that made sharing a locker room with players he had rooted for—such as Super Bowl XL MVP Hines Ward—a little surreal at first. "You're still fans of them, but now you're able to call them friends and brothers," Woodley said. "That's a great thing to be able to say, 'Now I can call Hines Ward,' or 'Hines Ward is giving me advice.'"

Woodley played behind Clark Haggans his rookie year while making the transition from a 4-3 college defensive end to a 3-4 outside linebacker. He broke out his second year with 11-and-a-half sacks and four fumble recoveries, and that does not include what he did in the postseason. Woodley had two sacks in the Steelers' three postseason games, including the one that ended Super Bowl XLIII.

What is crazier than Woodley starring for a squad he had once only rung up sacks for in a video game is that he emerged as an absolute game-wrecker while still learning Dick LeBeau's complex defense. "When I was out there, I can't say I knew every play," he said of the 2008 season. "I had a bunch of great veterans around me that helped me my second year in the league: Larry Foote, Deshea Townsend, Aaron Smith, who was on my left side and helped me get lined up sometimes," Woodley said. "Having those veteran guys consistently helping me helped me have a great sophomore year."

Woodley also thrived because of how at home he felt in Pittsburgh. "It was unique, not only from the players, but just the organization starting with Mr. [Dan] Rooney," he said of the late Steelers' owner. "They did a wonderful job making sure it was a family organization, and all of the players and secretaries, anybody that worked in that facility, we all knew one another. When you start creating bonds like that and you have Mr. Rooney coming down into the locker room and talking to guys, that's the kind of guys you want to represent your team for. When you join that, you're part of a brotherhood. You get to know the people that you're working with and you're going out there and playing with them on Sundays, and that bond and brotherhood was created across the board."

Outside linebackers like Woodley have long driven the Steelers' pressure defense, and the Steelers are usually at their best when those premier players come in pairs: James Harrison and Woodley, Greg Lloyd and Kevin Greene, and Jason Gildon and Joey Porter. Another pairing that Dick LeBeau puts with those duos during his time with the Steelers: Porter and Haggans.

The Steelers took Porter in the third round in the 1999 NFL Draft, and the Colorado State product blossomed into a star, making the NFL 2000s All-Decade Team and serving as the face of Pittsburgh's defense during much of that time. The Steelers did not have to look very far to find Porter a running mate. A year after they drafted Porter, they went back to Colorado State. There, they unearthed a gem in Haggans. He slipped into the fifth round of the 2000 draft despite setting the school record with 33 career sacks, a mark that still stands, and the Steelers were happy to grab him.

Haggans apprenticed under Gildon for four seasons before becoming a full-time starter in 2004, the year LeBeau returned to Pittsburgh for a second stint as the team's defensive coordinator. "Clark was very articulate, a quick learner, and an unusually fast player for his size," LeBeau recalled. "He was tailor-made for everything we were doing."

It did not take long for him to show it. He had six sacks in 2004 and nine in 2005, the season the Steelers won their fifth Super Bowl. Haggans recorded a sack in the Super Bowl, punctuating his breakout season. He and Porter played eight seasons together—only four when both were starters—and combined for 91 ½ sacks during that span. Haggans died on June 19, 2023, at the age of 46. The tributes that poured out remembered Haggans as much for the person he was as the player. "He was as good a teammate as you could ever ask for," LeBeau said, "and as good a man to coach as you could ever hope for."

—S.B.

19
Guardian Angels and a Super Finish

Back in the 1960s, the Pro Bowl was played in Los Angeles, and all the players looked forward to it. A good salary in the mid-1960s was $30,000 or $35,000, somewhere in that range. The winning team in the Pro Bowl got $7,000 per player, and the losing team got $5,000 per player, so we played pretty hard for the extra $2,000. That went a long way in the wintertime.

I played in three straight Pro Bowls from 1964 to 1966, and we were treated like celebrities in Los Angeles. The players who were out there for that game could go into all of these restaurants that had celebrity areas with Hollywood types. At one of the Pro Bowls, I was with Johnny Unitas and a couple of other guys, and we went into a restaurant and got ushered back to the celebrity room. We were sitting there, and Sammy Davis Jr. came in with about 14 people. Fifteen minutes into sitting around and getting ready to eat, Davis Jr. came over to our table and introduced himself as if we didn't know who the hell he was.

He was with people, who were going into a business venture together, but he sat down with us and was more interested in talking to the football players than he was being with the business folk. It was so cool because he was famous for his jewelry, and you should have seen the diamonds he had on his hands and the stickpin on his tie and his ears. I don't know what the monetary value was, but he was just glittering like gold. It made me think it would be good to have a Super Bowl ring some day.

I never got the opportunity to play for a Super Bowl ring and came up short in the big game the first three times I got there as a coach. While coaching for the Cincinnati Bengals, San Francisco 49ers quarterback Joe Montana beat us with late touchdown drives in 1982 and 1988. I got back to the Super Bowl in 1995 with the Pittsburgh Steelers, and we had a really good chance to win that game after falling behind early. In that Super Bowl XXX, the Dallas Cowboys started fast, scoring on their first two drives, putting up a touchdown and then a field goal to take a 10–0 lead. Our defense really settled in after that. Dallas, which had Hall of Famers throughout its lineup, managed just 140 yards of total offense the rest of the way. The Cowboys beat us 27–17, but their 254 yards of total offense had to be one of the lowest totals by a winning team in Super Bowl history.

As the 2000s progressed, I was beginning to get some longevity in my coaching career, and it's not like you're going to figure on getting to the Super Bowl five out of 10 years. I was thinking, *I'm going to go my whole career and never win one.* Then the 2005 season happened. The Steelers became the first team to make the Super Bowl as a sixth seed. Thanks to big plays like Willie Parker's 75-yard touchdown run and Hines Ward's 43-yard touchdown on a trick play, we held a 21–10 lead late when the Seattle Seahawks made a last-gasp drive. They were throwing every down, and we were just trying to get the game over without any big plays. They got down to our 23-yard line, and Matt Hasselbeck threw an incomplete pass. My mind was just going a mile a minute, thinking, *Fourth down coming up, what am I going to call? This is the Super Bowl! We've got to get them off the field here so there can't be any miracles.* The guys started going crazy around me after Hasselbeck's incomplete pass. I said, "What's wrong with you guys? They've got another down."

They said, "No, Coach, the game's over!"

I looked up at the scoreboard, and that had been fourth down. I was so involved in that situation that I lost track of the downs. At the end of the game, everybody left the field, and I just went over and sat down on our bench and I started at the scoreboard. I mean fixedly stared at it for minutes. I couldn't believe it. That was probably the most significant moment in coaching for me because I didn't want to coach all those years and never win a Super Bowl. That was one for the thumb for the Steelers, and, boy, did it feel great to be a part of the franchise's first Super Bowl win since the dynastic teams of the 1970s had won four Super Bowls.

Three years later we were back in the Super Bowl, and it might have had a mid-summer Latrobe, Pennsylvania, feel to it if both teams weren't playing on the world's biggest stage in Tampa, Florida. My good friend Ken Whisenhunt had guided the Arizona Cardinals to their first ever Super Bowl appearance in just his second season. We had recently matched wits for three years at training camp when he was the Steelers' offensive coordinator, and I was the defensive coordinator.

Whisenhunt was an excellent coach, and I knew his offense would be a handful. They had a Super Bowl-winning quarterback Kurt Warner and some excellent wide receivers led by Larry Fitzgerald and Anquan Boldin.

The game started really well for us after Arizona won the coin toss and deferred to the second half. We marched right down the field and got to their 1-yard line. Ben Roethlisberger ran a quarterback sneak, and the official signaled a touchdown. The Cardinals successfully challenged the call, and the ball was placed three inches from the goal line. Mike Tomlin took the points, and Jeff Reed's chip shot gave us a 3–0 lead.

We played really good defense in the first quarter, and our offense put together another long drive. This time we were able to bang it in from the 1-yard line with rookie running back Gary Russell scoring the touchdown that gave us a 10–0 lead a minute into the second quarter. We were doing everything we wanted to do in the game plan, especially keeping their offense off the field. The Cardinals tried running the ball early but couldn't do anything, so they just started passing. Just when it looked like we were in control of the game, a big play shifted momentum. Warner completed a 45-yard pass to Boldin to get the Cardinals going. He ran a post pattern, and we did not play outside in, and he got leverage to make the catch. Three plays later Warner threw a one-yard touchdown pass to pull the Cardinals to within 10–7.

The teams traded punts, and with a little more than two minutes left in the half, Roethlisberger had a ball tipped at the line of scrimmage. It was intercepted by Cardinals linebacker Karlos Dansby at our 34-yard line. Warner drove Arizona to our 2-yard line, where it had a first down with 18 seconds left in the half. We all figured he was going to throw it, so I called a max blitz. James Harrison's job was to make sure that nobody slid out of the line where they could pick up the free blitzer. He did and then played Warner's eyes. I don't think Warner ever saw him, and he just picked it off after a slight drop into coverage. When the Cardinals had started on our 34-yard line, I was hoping to get out of the half with our three-point lead intact. Then after they got near the goal line I said, "With a tie game, I'll be happy."

I was at the end of the coaches' box on our sidelines and probably on the field a little bit when Harrison made the interception. As he took off running, I yelled, "James, get down!" How many times have you seen a guy take off like that and fumble, and the other team gets the ball back?

He made a couple of cuts and made a couple of guys miss. Our guys were running over there just like we practiced in interceptions drills almost every day. When I saw there was a chance it could break, I started yelling, "Run, James, run!" Every block in that run was crucial, and that's only one reason why it's the greatest football play I've ever seen and the greatest play in Super Bowl history.

It was maybe 108 degrees on the field, and Harrison probably weighed around 260 pounds. It was solid muscle but still a lot of luggage to carry in that heat. He probably ran 150 yards on the play because he was weaving and jumping over people before crashing into the end zone. Fortunately, he was probably the best-conditioned athlete on our team, a well-known workout fiend. That allowed him to finish the play that defined this defense as well as anything. They did everything together. They were not going to let their brothers down. The same could be said of Harrison *after* that run.

A lesser-conditioned guy of that size would have been completely handicapped to continue playing football in the second half with energy and zest, but Harrison came out of the locker room like it was a brand-new day. He played as great a second half as you can ask in the football game. He kept his energy and his leverage and his pressure.

We kept the pressure on after Harrison's 100-yard interception return allowed us to take a 17–7 lead into the second half. We limited the Cardinals to 13 plays on their first two possessions in the third quarter. Our offense consumed half of the quarter with a 16-play drive that resulted in another short Reed field goal. That gave us a 20–7 lead with two minutes left in the third quarter. Unfortunately, it was kind of our high-water mark in terms of being in complete control of the game.

Warner started heating up and he took them on a good drive, one that covered 87 yards. It was all throwing, and a one-yard touchdown pass made it 20–14 with seven-and-half minutes to play. We went three-and-out, and they got the ball with 5:10 to go in the game. Warner was throwing the ball great, and they were moving the ball. A holding call forced them to punt, but we ended up pinned at the 1-yard line. I thought we could run three minutes off the clock, and if we got one more stop, we were going to be champions. It did not take long for those plans to get squashed. A holding penalty in the end zone gave the Cardinals a safety. With three minutes to play, we had to kick off to Arizona from our 20-yard line while clinging to a 20–16 lead.

Arizona took possession on its 36-yard line, and after an incomplete pass, I called for a four-man rush. They had Fitzgerald, and we had done a pretty good job on him until then. But Boldin was having a good day, and Steve Breaston, a kid from Pittsburgh, was having a good game, too. I wanted to give everybody help so I put everybody man under and the safeties deep. In that particular defense, you keep the guys out of the middle of the field, and we got beat over the middle by Fitzgerald, who's a great player and will be a first-ballot

Pro Football Hall of Famer. He was only about six yards downfield when he caught Warner's pass and he went straight up the middle for a 64-yard touchdown. He was faster than I thought he was, and that play featured the work of two great players: the quarterback and the wide receiver. We helped them a little, and those guys don't need any help. I was thinking on the sideline, *Man, there's this beautiful defense that played all these great games, and now it looks like we're going to blow it with that damn pass that Fitzgerald caught.*

I felt sick, and that's when I turned to my guardian angels: Roethlisberger and Santonio Holmes. I was raised Presbyterian, and every Sunday we all went to church. Afterward we would go down to my grandmother's house and eat a big dinner of chicken, mashed potatoes, green beans, rolls, and salad. Our little church sat on Elm Street in London, Ohio, and some people would park on the side of the street for the service. My grandmother—I can remember this like yesterday, even though it happened in the 1940s—said she almost got killed one day. The church had about 15 steps that came down out of the front door of the church to a sidewalk, and then there were the parking spaces that went right along the street. You didn't really have much vision when you were stepping out between those parked cars.

My grandmother was a little bit distracted in thought and was walking in between two of the parked cars. For some reason, she could not take another step and froze before crossing the street. Ten seconds later a car went whipping by and was going 30 miles an hour, and it would have seemed like 100 if you were standing right beside it. It would have splattered her, and that's how close she came to meeting her demise that morning. I can still hear her sitting at that dinner table, saying, "I know for sure it was my guardian angel that just held me back. I was just powerless to move and I wanted to cross." I've always carried that thought. There have been other instances of people talking about the supernatural. That incident made me feel a little closer to the almighty and the high and mighty. That's what I think happened to the defense down in Tampa Bay. Roethlisberger and Holmes prevented our season for the ages from getting splattered at Raymond James Stadium.

We only needed a field goal to tie the game at 23, and to some that may have looked like a best-case scenario after a holding penalty on our first play. That came after Arizona's touchdown backed us up to our 12-yard line with 2:24 left in the game. I never gave up on the offense because I had seen Roethlisberger thrive in these situations so many times. Sure enough, he and Holmes started playing pitch and catch like they were in the backyard.

The big play came when Roethlisberger hit Holmes on a simple hook pattern, and he pulled out the backdoor, leaving several defenders grasping for air. He raced all the way to the Arizona 6-yard line on the 40-yard catch and run with 50 seconds left. Two plays later, they delivered a second iconic Super Bowl play in the same game. Roethlisberger dropped back, and I saw three Cardinals defenders where he was looking in the right corner of the end zone. Roethlisberger started winding up, and I said to myself, "Oh, Ben, don't throw that." I knew we had more downs and could kick a field goal if we did not score a touchdown.

Roethlisberger let it rip, and that ball was humming. The vertical leap that Holmes exhibited getting up for that ball and the accuracy of Roethlisberger to fit it into the corner of the end zone so perfectly was incredible. We practiced stuff like that in the red zone period every week, but you only get execution like that once every 10 years—even at the NFL level. It was the damndest catch that I've ever seen. To this day, mention Holmes' name, and I see that play. You talk about hand/eye coordination at the perfect moment. When Holmes came down, his feet were only in by about two inches. A review confirmed the touchdown. I've looked at the video over and over and I still don't know how Holmes caught that ball. Several things in that game were meant to be, and that's my guardian angel shining on us that night through Holmes and Roethlisberger.

We had the lead 27–23 with 35 seconds to play, but I was worried. We had just given them a 64-yard touchdown. We had to find a way to get off the field and win this Super Bowl. When they went out the last time, nothing had to be said. All I did was tell them the game situation.

Warner, still red-hot, hit Fitzgerald on a crossing pattern for 20 yards, which put Arizona on its own 43-yard line. After a timeout Warner completed a 13-yard pass to running back J.J. Arrington to get the Cardinals into our territory. They called their final timeout with 15 seconds left to play. I didn't normally like playing three-man rushes, but with time a factor, I said, "I've got to play the percentages." We rushed three, and LaMarr Woodley did not beat his man clean, but he kept working. He hit Warner, and the ball popped out. Brett Keisel recovered it. I could finally relax.

It was a heck of a way to end our season and probably fitting, too. Just as they had all season, players stepped up on both sides of the ball. Nothing illustrated that more than Harrison's interception return for a touchdown and Roethlisberger and Holmes' Immaculate Connection that secured the Steelers' sixth Super Bowl win. What we accomplished during the 2008 season really hit me during our victory parade a couple weeks later in downtown Pittsburgh. People were hanging off streetlights. They were climbing trees. They were on roofs as far as you could see. It was an absolute sea of people and it was all about the Pittsburgh Steelers winning the Super Bowl. Troy Polamalu got out in the crowd and body surfed. I was thinking, *Be careful with my safety!* Those images will be forever fixed in my mind.

Almost three months later, we visited the White House and met with president Barack Obama. We got to visit with the president and took a team picture with him in the White House press room. We adjourned to the South Lawn of the White House where we helped prepare care packages for those serving in the military. The president started calling out different players and then he said, "Where's Dick LeBeau?" I waved, and he said, "Everybody knows Dick LeBeau." The enormity of the situation was overwhelming. I thought to myself, *Man, this is a long way from London, Ohio.*

There was no place I would have rather been—not because of the setting so much but the people that were there with me. The coaches, the players, people throughout the organization had all played a role in a truly special season. That was a great thing to experience and have it come out the way it did. What made that year particularly outstanding was our defense had such a great statistical season and then ended up being world champions. I'll never forget them. And what they accomplished.

Super Stars

The Pittsburgh Steelers, aided by James Harrison's 100-yard interception return for a touchdown at the end of the first half, took a 20–7 lead into the fourth quarter of Super Bowl XLIII. They seemed to be firmly in control.

Someone forgot to tell Arizona quarterback Kurt Warner and wide receiver Larry Fitzgerald that the upstart Cardinals were finished. Warner and Fitzgerald were just getting started. The two hooked up for a pair of touchdowns in the final quarter as the Cardinals scored 16 unanswered points to vault ahead of the Steelers 23–20.

Particularly galling to a group that rarely gave up big plays was the 64-yard touchdown Fitzgerald scored after catching a short pass and then streaking right through the heart of the Steelers' defense. Fitzgerald's touchdown came with just 2:47 minutes to play, capping a stunning reversal of fortune. "I was about to cry," safety Ryan Clark said.

"I was like, damn, we just lost this game," Harrison said.

Ben Roethlisberger and Santonio Holmes had other ideas. And in poker parlance, they saw Warner and Fitzgerald's brilliance and raised them, though only after an early hiccup with the season on the line. "First play of the drive I remember going in the huddle and I tried to pull a Joe Montana/John Candy story moment and tell the guys and calm them down, and first play we get a [holding] penalty," Roethlisberger recalled. "I was like, boy, that sure didn't work. We got out of the hole and moved down the field."

He and Holmes hooked up for completions of 13, 14, and 40 yards to set up the Steelers at the Arizona 6-yard line with 48 seconds to play. They appeared to connect on the next play for the go-ahead touchdown, but Holmes could not hang onto the pass in the left corner of the end zone. That merely set the stage for the one of the greatest plays in Super Bowl history. Roethlisberger threw a pass in the right corner of the end zone that just cleared the hands of several Cardinals defensive backs. Holmes made a toe-tapping catch for the dramatic touchdown. "The catch that Holmes made was spectacular," Roethlisberger said. "We joke—and I've heard it a thousand times—the pass before on the other side of the end zone would have been a lot easier, but it was one of those times and plays that will forever live in all of our minds and our hearts. I threw that ball and I wasn't quite sure what was going to happen, but thank the Lord it got over everybody's hands, and Holmes was able to catch it."

The Steelers defense made the most of its reprieve, and a LaMarr Woodley sack and Brett Keisel fumble recovery ended the game.

"We are forever grateful to Ben Roethlisberger and Santonio Holmes," Clark said. "We were a team, and I think without the ensuing drive the defense clearly isn't remembered the way it is. Without that drive we aren't champions, and it's our fault that we aren't."

What was almost as gratifying for Roethlisberger as winning a second Super Bowl before his 28th birthday was how the offense had picked up the defense the one time it needed it. "That defense had played so well all year, and they were going to go down in the history books as one of the great defenses of all time," Roethlisberger said. "If you lose the Super Bowl, they still were great, but people will say, 'Yeah, but they lost.' For us to go out there and find a way to get down the field and score, it really meant the world to us as an offense because that defense had carried us so much throughout the year. We were a good offense, too, but they were something on a different level."

The defense—particularly Woodley—did finish things off. He sacked Warner on the final play of the game, causing a fumble that Keisel pounced on, preserving Pittsburgh's wild 27–23 win. Then Keisel pulled a veteran move. "The confetti's coming down, we celebrating, and he comes up to me and says, 'Woodley, do you want the ball?'" Woodley said, laughing. "So he caught me at the right time."

At that time Woodley was so caught up in the moment that he said no. Keisel still has the ball and he does not dispute Woodley's account of what happened right after the Steelers won their sixth Super Bowl. What he points out is that he *did* offer the keepsake to Woodley—only for Woodley to tell him to keep it. "Now he gives me hell about it," Keisel said, laughing.

Fair warning for Keisel: Woodley is still stalking that ball as he once did quarterbacks. "If I ever have a chance to go over to Brett Keisel's house, which he won't let me come over, I'm getting that ball," Woodley said. "LaMarr's on the hunt for the ball!"

—G.V.B.

Afterword

A Super Bowl that produced great plays by great players also treated a worldwide audience to a wild finish in Tampa, Florida. It caused heart palpitations for both fan bases and ultimately heartbreak for one of them. The Pittsburgh Steelers held off the Arizona Cardinals 27–23 behind two iconic plays in the same Super Bowl, winning their sixth Lombardi Trophy. Then, linebacker LaMarr Woodley ended the drama with a sack. "Thank God for Woodley making the sack caused fumble," safety Troy Polamalu said, "because the last thing that I envisioned was Larry Fitzgerald Randy Mossing us in the end zone."

But one surreal moment remained. While celebrating their win against the Cardinals, Steelers players, coaches, and personnel formed two lines leading to the riser on the field at Raymond James Stadium. There, NFL commissioner Roger Goodell presented Steelers owner Dan Rooney, team president Art Rooney II, and head coach Mike Tomlin with the Lombardi Trophy.

Delivering the trophy to Goodell was Joe Willie Namath, who knew a thing or two about Super Bowl heroics. "Broadway Joe" was wearing an oversized fur coat on a humid South Florida evening because, of course, he was. As he made his way through the Steelers' lines, Namath spied Dick LeBeau standing between defensive ends Aaron Smith and Brett Keisel. Namath walked up to the coordinator of a defense that had authored a season worthy of Steel Curtain lore. Without a word he kissed LeBeau on the cheek and then continued toward the riser. "I thought to myself, *Well, this has been quite a day. We win the Super Bowl in a hell of a game, and I get kissed by Joe Namath,*" LeBeau said with a laugh.

Unexpected as the gesture was, it provided a perfect metaphor for how LeBeau felt about his players. He loved his "guys," as he *still* calls them, and could not have been happier for them after a Super Bowl for the ages. LeBeau would not have loved them any less had the Steelers fallen short on this wild night. But he would have been crushed—for them. He had crunched the numbers from the 2008 regular season, when the Steelers' defense led the NFL in almost every major statistical category. Those numbers were otherworldly, especially in an era of pass-happy offenses. But LeBeau knows as well as anyone how harshly history can judge. Had the Steelers not won the Super Bowl, the defense he would put up against any in NFL history would not have been remembered in the light he knew it deserved. Or as James Harrison put it, as only the 2008 NFL Defensive Player of the Year could: "When it came down to it, it don't matter what the defense did. Were we the ones that were hoisting up the Lombardi? That's all that matters. Only one team succeeds every year. Everybody else fails."

Fortunately for the Steelers, they were able to finish what they started in 2008. It wasn't perfect. It wasn't always pretty. But their body of work cemented the team's place in history. That is especially true of the defense. It had everything: size, speed, depth, playmakers at every level. And what made the unit transcendent was the trust the players had in their coach and each other. That nurtured an ethos that defined the defense as much as one of Polamalu's how-did-he-do-that interceptions or Harrison barreling around a corner and bearing down on some unfortunate quarterback. Simply put: the players never wanted to let down their brothers or their defensive coordinator. Especially their defensive coordinator.

LeBeau wasn't a father figure to them. He *was* a father to them. "When I look at that group, it was a bunch of kids that just liked each other and loved playing," said Aaron Smith, who since retiring from the NFL has coached high school boys basketball in the Pittsburgh area. "As I coach now, I say, 'Listen, guys, I played on some good teams. But the 2008 team, we didn't care who it was or where it was. If we were together, we could beat anybody.' As a group we weren't in fear of anybody. We knew that we had the belief in each other that we could get it done as a group. There were teams that individually had better players, but collectively I don't think you would have found a group more willing to fight for each other than that group."

That is the effect LeBeau has on people. It makes him every bit as unique as the 59 years he spent in the NFL: 14 as a player, 45 as a coach. "Every offseason Coach LeBeau would tell us he loved us and thank us for letting him be our coach," said safety Ryan Clark, who is now an NFL analyst for ESPN. "I would always think to myself, *One, clearly Coach LeBeau has no idea who he is or how we love him and think of him.* But that level of humility to love his players and his job and to be so grateful that he would thank people for allowing the greatest defensive coach in history of football to coach them just said everything that could be said."

Sixteen years later that group is still connected in every way imaginable. Sometimes, when feeling nostalgic, Brett Keisel will call LeBeau with explicit instructions: "Just say 'fire zone' to me one time or 'alert falcon closed zebra wide.' Just say that to me so I can hear that again."

It was a magical time, one all involved with would have bottled, starting with LeBeau. Time, however, marches on. Memories are the one concession it makes. That is what moved James Farrior to happy tears a decade after he had captained some great Steelers defenses, including the 2008 outfit. Living in Los Angeles with his wife and four kids, he received a card in the mail. It was from LeBeau. Handwritten, it thanked Farrior for everything he had done and saying how much he has meant to LeBeau. "It was just out of the blue," Farrior said of the card that he kept on his nightstand for years. "I was crying like a baby."

LeBeau is not an overly emotional person. His guys, though, could make him cry. After the 2008 season, they gave him a gold Rolex watch. From the sheer cost of the gift to the meaning behind it, the gesture overwhelmed LeBeau. "I've never heard of a coach getting that kind of gift from his team," he said. "It's more valuable than every piece of clothing that I have. It's one of my most prized possessions."

The watch is so precious to LeBeau that he won't even wear it. Indeed, he keeps it in a safety deposit box at a bank. It is one of many concrete links between LeBeau and the players from the Steelers' 2008 defense—like the Lombardi Trophy and across-the-board statistics that LeBeau is not sure will ever again be matched, much less exceeded. But when looking back at that group, that time, what matters most to LeBeau is what endures in everyone's hearts. "We had an exceptional bunch of coaches and we had an even more exceptional bunch of players," LeBeau said. "They treated me with a tremendous amount of respect, and sometimes it was humbling how well they treated me and responded to my coaching. They were close and they're close today and they'll be close as long as two of them are left on the Earth because of the bond that they built and the standard that they set for each other."

—S.B.

Appendix I: Author Tributes

Two Dick LeBeau memories from when I covered the Pittsburgh Steelers stand out above others. The first one was the week after the Steelers beat the Baltimore Ravens in the 2008 AFC Championship game to advance to the Super Bowl. Toward the end of an exhausting week for me of churning out pre-Super Bowl copy for the *Pittsburgh Tribune-Review*, LeBeau walked into the media room at the Steelers' practice facility.

Instead of standing at the podium to field questions, he took a seat. Arguably the greatest NFL defensive coordinator of all time proceeded to talk about the 2008 defense, breaking down the numbers and making the case—check that, confirming—of its historical transcendence. It was...surreal, like Kissinger talking foreign policy. The only thing missing was a glowing fireplace behind LeBeau.

Fast forward nine months. The Steelers, coming off the Super Bowl victory that gave them a sixth Lombardi Trophy, had just beaten the Detroit Lions, the team LeBeau had starred for as a cornerback for 14 seasons, 28–20. The defense had given up at least 20 points for the second straight game. Something seemed off. Had teams figured out the great Steelers defense—and by extension LeBeau? When he met with reporters four days later, questions weren't framed as such, but they may have nibbled at those edges. LeBeau got a little testy during the session though, of course, he never raised his voice. Afterward, I had a weird feeling while walking away with other reporters. I could not quite place it. That is when Ken Laird, a talented radio personality, voiced what I and probably others were thinking. "I feel like my dad just yelled at me," Laird said.

There it was, and it was something that made reporters at that moment no different than players like Troy Polamalu, James Harrison, James Farrior, and countless others. As much as our job was to ask tough questions, we did not want to disappoint LeBeau.

What happened on May 4, 2023, as George Von Benko and I were working on this book, is one of countless reasons why. Coach and I had scheduled a phone interview for 9:00 PM. We connected around 9:15, and he apologized profusely. His nine-hole golf league had run long—in fact his group was finishing in darkness—and he said he would call me a little later. I could not believe what he told me after we re-connected.

The nine holes had taken three-and-a-half hours. Anyone who has played golf knows that is an absurd amount of time; most would have been anywhere from extremely annoyed to furious. Not LeBeau. He shrugged it off as a kink from the first night of the league, something that would be worked out. Besides, he said, he got to play the game he loves with his son, Brandon. As he drove home with his wife, Nancy, he stopped at a local McDonald's to pick up a late dinner. We put the interview on hold as he hit the drive-through, but I stayed on the line. A young lady took the order and then talked about how excited she was for her upcoming prom. They chatted her up about it and told her to have a great time. The conversation was so easy, the LeBeaus' happiness for the young girl so genuine. Something utterly mundane struck me as something more, a glimpse at the man behind the legend. In its own way, it tied everything together while working on this book with LeBeau.

The beauty of the 2008 Steelers…an endless round of golf…a Quarter Pounder with only lettuce, tomatoes, and mayonnaise. Three things should have had nothing to do with each other. And yet they *are* Dick

LeBeau. As a coach and a person. I'm not sure we will ever see another one like him.

Steelers director of football operations Tom Donahoe found himself a regular eavesdropper when he roomed across the hall from Dom Capers during training camp in 1992. Yes, even top executives stay in the dormitories while the Steelers summer at St. Vincent College in Latrobe, Pennsylvania. And, no, Donahoe was not spying. He had been a successful high school coach before moving into scouting. Even after rising to the highest of NFL ranks, he remained a teacher—and seeker of knowledge—at heart. He often stationed himself outside of Capers' room at night just to soak in the Steelers' defensive coordinator talking shop with the team's first-year defensive backs coach.

That first-year coach? LeBeau. "It was fascinating because the two of them had a great relationship, and a lot of things we did defensively were a product of Coach LeBeau," Donahoe said. "Dick was really instrumental to me in my career learning about defensive football, zone blitz, game planning."

Year later, after LeBeau had succeeded Capers as the Steelers' defensive coordinator, Donahoe sometimes sat in on his meetings. "Just to watch him interact with the players, watch him teach, and, for my benefit, learn football," Donahoe said, "there's nobody better with people than Dick LeBeau. I'm honored to call him a really close friend."

Donahoe was the last person we talked to for this book. He, like everyone else we interviewed, could not say enough about LeBeau. There are about 1,937 reasons why, and that includes LeBeau's humility. He was adamant that the focus be on the 2008 Steelers defense—specifically the players who powered the franchise to its sixth Super Bowl title. There were several problems with these parameters. One, you cannot tell a story about the 2008 Steelers, or the NFL for that matter, without LeBeau's own story. Even more problematic was his players were as enthusiastic to talk about him as he was about them.

The book, as a result, is something of a compromise. It is about a defense unlike any other LeBeau ever coached—and a season that ended with the Steelers hoisting a sixth Lombardi Trophy. Woven throughout it is LeBeau's story. It is hardly all of it; a book on just him would have been a hard no from the subject himself. But we would have had to answer to James Harrison (among others) if there was not any of LeBeau in this book. So, there you go, Coach.

That brings us to the many people who made telling this story possible. That starts with LeBeau. He was so committed to giving the 2008 Steelers their due that he went back and watched every game from a season that is still fresh in his mind. He reviewed them in detail with us, also answering questions we had during interviews that often stretched past three hours.

Others were just as giving with their time, especially the players on the 2008 defense. We cannot thank enough the following for interviews: Ryan Clark, James Farrior, Larry Foote, Casey Hampton, Chris Hoke, Harrison, Brett Keisel, Bryant McFadden, Troy Polamalu, Aaron Smith, Ike Taylor, Deshea Townsend, and LaMarr Woodley.

Thanks to Kevin Colbert, Donahoe, Bill Priatko, and Ben Roethlisberger. They were also generous in sharing their experiences with LeBeau.

We are grateful to the Pittsburgh Steelers—especially Burt Lauten, Michael Bertsch, and Karl Rosner—for their help with interviews and photos and their enthusiasm for this project. Also thank you to Bill Keenist of the Detroit Lions and Karen Dertinger of Ohio State for assisting us with photos of Coach LeBeau before he was, well, Coach LeBeau.

Finally, thank you to Triumph Books, especially Tom Bast and Jeff Fedotin. Tom embraced this idea from the start, and Jeff made it happen with his skillful editing and bottomless reservoir of patience with us.

—S.B.

I first became aware of Dick LeBeau as a young football fan in the 1960s when he was a defensive back for the Detroit Lions. I watched him play on television many times, especially the Thanksgiving Day game in Detroit that usually had the Lions facing the Green Bay Packers. I collected football cards and had many LeBeau cards in my collection.

I started in radio when I was 15 years old and began covering the Pittsburgh Steelers. I covered my first Steelers training camp in 1969. That was Chuck Noll's first year as head coach. I saw the Steel Curtain and was blessed to be in attendance at the first Super Bowl the Steelers played in. LeBeau began a defensive assistant tenure for the Steelers in 1992, and I had several interviews with him during this period. He left in 1997 and returned to Pittsburgh as defensive coordinator in 2004.

I developed a strong friendship with Coach LeBeau through a mutual friend Bill Priatko, who was LeBeau's first NFL roommate after he was drafted by the Cleveland Browns in 1959. The friendship grew over the years, and on many occasions during the football season, I would have lunch with LeBeau and Priatko at the Steelers' practice facility on the south side of Pittsburgh. Those were great times filled with great football talk.

At one point I had formed a company with my friend, Chuck Greenwood, that conducted autograph signings with athletes. One signing we did was with LeBeau and some of his Detroit teammates: Milt Plum, Roger Brown, and Jim Gibbons. LeBeau has been a frequent guest on my sports talk show. He always gave me time, and I recall sitting with him at Super Bowl media sessions. These are tremendous memories.

I cherish my friendship with Dick LeBeau. He is one of the best people I have ever met in the world of sports and life in general. I can honestly say in my 50-plus years covering sports, I have never met a coach who was loved by his players like LeBeau was.

—G.V.B.

Appendix II: The 2008 Pittsburgh Steelers Defense

NT Casey Hampton—"You gotta have an outstanding nose tackle to play the point of that odd man front. Hampton was unblockable and he anchored the whole thing around the defensive line."

DE Aaron Smith—"I could count on the fingers of one hand how many times he got blocked in a year. He never was out of his gap and he never took the wrong side of the offensive player. He was 99.9 percent grading out every week."

DE Brett Keisel—"He was one of the hardest-working players I ever had the honor to coach. He was a tremendous athlete. You couldn't run at him, and he was fast enough [that] if you ran away from him he was probably going to get in on that tackle, too."

DL Chris Hoke—"Hoke was Mr. Dependable for us. He played all of the positions on the line, was an excellent nose tackle. In that year I think Hampton missed parts or all of several games, and the defense never missed a beat with Hoke handling his part expertly."

OLB LaMarr Woodley—"We drafted Woodley because of his pass-rushing skills. He had really been a defensive end at Michigan. In his second or third preseason game as a rookie, he covered a tight end and knocked the pass away. I turned to coach Keith Butler and said, 'We don't have to worry about him. He is going to be fine.'"

OLB James Harrison—"Harrison won the Defensive Player of the Year in the league in 2008. He probably had it won four weeks before the season was over with the numbers he put up. His interception in that Super Bowl game and return for a touchdown on the last play before halftime is the best football play I've ever seen."

MLB James Farrior—"Farrior was our defensive captain and he was the leader of our defense. One of the most vocal positive leaders that I've ever been around, I don't know that he ever got the proper acclaim that he should have gotten for how good a player that he was. He was definitely one of the best linebackers that played in the NFL."

MLB Larry Foote—"Foote was like having a coach on the field. He knew everybody's assignment and he was an excellent communicator and was always very, very positive."

LB Lawrence Timmons—"Timmons had a great professional career. We were stacked at linebacker, and he kind of worked his way into the NFL without having to carry the whole load that first year. He was very productive and was a contributor."

SS Troy Polamalu—"When you start naming the best of all time at this position, it's pretty hard not to start with him at safety. He was a safety who could play corner. There's not an area for a football player that he didn't excel in: running, change of direction, tackling, intelligence, competitiveness, and he was one of those guys who had the knack and ability to come up with the biggest plays at the most important times."

FS Ryan Clark—"He was probably as close to contributing to Polamalu's success as any player. The two of them were a perfect tandem, and I'm not saying it was telepathic, but I never saw them talking, but somehow they always got the message out to each other where they were going to be."

CB Ike Taylor—"Taylor was a great competitor and he loved to have a tough assignment and invariably he would complete the assignment he was given."

CB Bryant McFadden—"We drafted him out of Florida State. Deshea Townsend had a nagging injury that was prolonged. McFadden had to play an awful lot of football. He proved his value over and over again."

DB Deshea Townsend—"Townsend and Foote have gone on to coaching careers in the NFL. Deshea was just like having a coach on the field. He knew everybody's assignment and could execute his with intelligence and balance as good as anyone I ever coached."

DB Tyrone Carter—"He was a veteran player and had a lot of playing time in the NFL. He was an invaluable non-starter, and you didn't lose anything when he was playing."

DL Nick Eason—"In our base defense, we have three lineman that play and, when teams went to four wide receivers, we would get into a four-lineman front, and you have to have depth in the defensive line. Eason could fill the role for depth, and he was like a starter when he was in there."

DL Travis Kirschke—"Kirschke was a great acquisition for us, and we had some injuries in the defensive line that year, and Kirschke had to play more than one position. He and Hoke never quit on one down. They optimized the defense."

LB Keyaron Fox—"He was a tremendous special teams player and he gave us good depth."

LB Patrick Bailey—"Bailey was the same as Fox. They were huge contributors to our special teams and they made a difference when they were under kicks because they were skilled linebackers. They both could also play very well from scrimmage."

LB Bruce Davis—"Davis was a good hardworking player with an excellent college reputation, and that was reflected in his high draft choice. He contributed in many ways to the defensive success. The simple truth is with the guys that we had the depth of talent was such that they couldn't all play, and Davis got caught in that situation."

DB Fernando Bryant—"We had some injuries and we picked him up in the middle of the season, and he made two plays in a tight game in the end zone, and I'll never forget that. Again, you had a veteran player used to defending in key situations."

LB Andre Frazier—"I coached his dad in Cincinnati, and Andre was a very active aggressive player and competitor like his dad."

DB William Gay—"Gay was a big contributor to our defense for many years. The more important the situation was in the game, the more likely Gay was going to come up with the play. He had a great career."

DB Roy Lewis—"We picked Lewis up as a free agent from the University of Washington, and he was active on the special teams side of things. He was a real solid tackler and an aggressive player."

DB Anthony Madison—"Madison was a good corner. Corner is like defensive line. You can't go through an NFL season without excellent depth. Madison came through for us. He was a depth guy who played a lot of football."

DT Scott Paxson—"Paxson was a tremendous competitor and had a great collegiate career at Penn State. We loved getting players from local schools."

DE Orpheus Roye—"We had him before, and he went to Cleveland and played. When we had injuries, we picked him up, and when we got him, he had to play. He knew the defense, and we knew he would take care of business, and that is what he did."

S Anthony Smith—"He was a high draft pick from Syracuse. He was a very solid safety and played a lot of football for us. He was very aggressive."

LB Donovan Woods—"He was a free-agent linebacker from Oklahoma State. He played special teams and was a good support player."

About the Authors

Dick LeBeau spent 59 seasons in the NFL—14 as a player with the Detroit Lions and 45 as a coach. He coached for the Pittsburgh Steelers from 1992 to 1996 and from 2004 to 2014. Twice with LeBeau as their defensive coordinator, the Steelers won the Super Bowl, including in 2008, and appeared in it two other times. He also had coaching stints with the Philadelphia Eagles, Green Bay Packers, Cincinnati Bengals, Buffalo Bills, and Tennessee Titans. LeBeau, whose 62 career interceptions are tied for 10th most in NFL history, is in the Pro Football Hall of Fame. LeBeau lives in Montgomery, Ohio, with his wife Nancy.

Scott Brown covered the Steelers from 2006 to 2014 for the *Pittsburgh Tribune-Review* and ESPN.com. He has written nine other books, including *In the Locker Room* with Tunch Ilkin, *The Pittsburgh Steelers' Fans Bucket List*, and *Miracle in the Making: The Adam Taliaferro Story.* His book *The Reggie Warford Story: Integrating Basketball at the University of Kentucky* will be published in November 2024 by the University Press of Kentucky. Brown is the site editor of Steelers Depot and lives in Greensburg, Pennsylvania.

George Von Benko has been a fixture on the Western Pennsylvania sports scene since he started his broadcasting career at the age of 15. In his 57-year journey through the sports world, he has broadcast college football and basketball and been a longtime voice of sports talk radio. His first year covering the Pittsburgh Steelers in 1969 was also Chuck Noll's first year as the team's head coach. Von Benko has written three books: *Memory Lane*, *Memory Lane Vol. 2*, and *Sports Talk*. Von Benko, whose *Sports Line* show can be heard every Saturday morning on WMBS Radio, lives in Connellsville, Pennsylvania.